QUOTATIONS
OF WIT AND
WISDOM:
Know or
Listen to
Those Who Know

QUOTATIONS OF WIT AND WISDOM:

Know or Listen to Those Who Know

⌇ ⌇ ⌇

John W. Gardner &

Francesca Gardner Reese

W · W · NORTON & COMPANY · INC ·

NEW YORK LONDON

First published as a Norton paperback 1980; reissued 1996.

Library of Congress Cataloging in Publication Data
Main entry under title:
Quotations of Wit and Wisdom:
Know or Listen to Those Who Know
Includes index.
1. Quotations, English.   I. Gardner, John William,
    1912–   II. Reese, Francesca Gardner.
PN6081.K55   808.88′2   75-19328

ISBN 0-393-31446-4

W. W. Norton & Company, Inc.
500 Fifth Avenue, New York, N.Y. 10110
W. W. Norton & Company Ltd.
10 Coptic Street, London WC1A 1PU

1 2 3 4 5 6 7 8 9 0

A la muy querida
DOÑA CARLOTA
quien sabía
y también supo escuchar

CONTENTS

INTRODUCTION

Y father and I put this book together for the pleasure
it gave us. We hoped from the beginning that it
would please others, but we saw that as a chancier
thing. Robinson Jeffers once said of poetry, "If you like it,
listen to it; if not, let it alone." This is not a volume of
poetry, but the suggestion applies. Read it for pleasure or
put it down. It is not a reference work. It is not adult education. It is for your enjoyment.

One more thing—while I'm in the flood tide of saying
what the book isn't—it isn't a compendium of ideas of
which we approve. Even had we been tempted to make it
such, we could never have agreed between us on the items
that earned our approval. In any case, we saw merit and
stimulus in giving space to the memorable expression of ideas
wholly at odds with our own. Whitman said, "Have you
not learned great lessons from those who . . . dispute the
passage with you?"

Sometimes a quotation commended itself to us because
there was an original idea embedded in it. Others appealed
to us on the ground of imagination. Or wit. Or historical
interest. Or a sharp eye for the ridiculous.

It would be nice to be able to say that all of the quotations here express truths that have stood the test of time. But
it's not a safe assertion, and certainly not a modest one. First
of all, we have no special divining rod that locates truth.
Besides, the book contains many aphorisms, and it is a
sprightly flaw of the aphorism that it is almost always

slightly untrue. In order to retain its brevity and bite, it shears away qualifying clauses, shuns tentativeness, and buys vividness at the cost of precision.

Having expressed these cautions, we are willing to say we think the book is richly laden with statements that are both wise and true.

For the reader well grounded in history and literature, there will be few unfamiliar names among our authors. But we would like to think that even the well-grounded reader will be tempted to go back to the original authors: to Whitehead, the great English philosopher and mathematician who moved to the United States at the age of sixty-three and lit our sky for another twenty-three years; to Montaigne, the great sixteenth-century essayist, who should be revisited periodically by every civilized person; to William James, whose humane warmth and sparkle outshone both his philosophic and psychological contributions; to H. F. Amiel, the obscure Swiss diarist who observed his century with unrivaled sensitivity; to Loren Eiseley, contemporary anthropologist, whose writings will be treasured long after most of today's literary figures are forgotten; to Balthasar Gracian, the extraordinary seventeenth-century Spanish Jesuit who made an art form of the maxim.

A word must be said concerning the substantial number of items that are pessimistic or at least bleakly realistic in tone or substance. Neither of the editors is melancholy by temperament. But since long before Ecclesiastes, memorable bursts of language have dealt more often with rascality than with virtue, more often with harsh truths than with redeeming visions. Proverbs are apt to be especially down-to-earth. They offer very little of Pollyanna and a great deal of life with the bark off. Mostly, they deal unblinkingly with human flaws and foolishness, tragedy, everyday head-bumpings, and the shirt-sleeved cynicism of daily life.

Proverbs present a problem of attribution. The great proverbs have been great travelers. They show up in many languages in virtually the same form. For many proverbs this polyglottal range dates from the long period when Latin was the scholar's language for all of Europe. Given that circumstance it is often wholly arbitrary to identify a particular proverb as "German" or "Italian" or "English." It's not a problem that kept us awake nights, but it seems worth mentioning. Thomas Fuller and John Ray were collectors of proverbs who published compendiums in the seventeenth and eighteenth centuries. We have attached their names to the items drawn from their collections.

In the case of Latin, French, Italian, German, and Spanish proverbs, we have checked (or made) the translations ourselves. But we do not have a command of other languages. Proverbs we cite from other languages may, for all we know, have suffered or gained in the translation.

Kierkegaard said, "Life must be understood backward." This book can be understood backward, forward, or sideways. Start in the middle if that is your impulse.

You will probably have more pleasure from the entries if you read no more than a few at one sitting. Linger over them. If it's your habit to race through a book, try a change of pace. Ease into it with a pleasantly dilatory shuffle. Loiter. Dawdle. Enjoy.

Francesca Gardner Reese

ACKNOWLEDGMENTS

WE ARE grateful to Mary Hanson, Cynthia Hahn, and John Wood for their wholehearted assistance; to Vicki and John Salmon for help in verifying some of the quotations; and to all our family and friends who helped and encouraged us.

ONE

Portraits in Words

"A Glimpse of the Everlasting Granite"

Hawthorne isn't a handsome man, nor an engaging one personally. He has the look all the time, to one who doesn't know him, of a rogue who suddenly finds himself in a company of detectives. But in spite of his rusticity, I felt a sympathy with him amounting to anguish, and couldn't take my eyes off him all the dinner. . . . The old world is breaking up on all hands—the glimpse of the everlasting granite I caught in Hawthorne shows that there is stock enough for fifty better.

Henry James, Sr.

When God made Carl, he didn't do anything else that day.

Edward Steichen
(speaking of Carl Sandburg)

Harding was not a bad man. He was just a slob.

Alice Roosevelt Longworth

He soared to the infinite and dived into the unfathomable, but never paid cash.

Anonymous description of Bronson Alcott

I don't object to the old man keeping a card up his sleeve, but I do object to his asserting that God put it there.

Henry Labouchère
(speaking of W. E. Gladstone)

He was a bad lawyer, . . . but he was the most sensible looking man talking nonsense I ever saw.

Daniel O'Connell
(speaking of Lord Manners)

Poor Matt, he's gone to Heaven, no doubt—but he won't like God.

Robert Louis Stevenson
(on hearing of Matthew Arnold's death)

When Byron's eyes were shut in death,
We bow'd our head and held our breath.
He taught us little: but our soul
Had *felt* him like the thunder's roll.

Matthew Arnold

Mad, bad, and dangerous to know.

Lady Caroline Lamb
(speaking of Byron)

That wonderful Edward Coke was loose—masterful, masterless man.

Frederic W. Maitland

The Chief Justice was rich, quiet, and infamous.

Thomas Macaulay
(speaking of Warren Hastings)

Young froths and foams and bubbles, sometimes very vigorously; but we must not compare the noise made by your teakettle here with the roaring of the ocean.

Samuel Johnson
(to one who compared the poet Edward Young
to Shakespeare)

Father, being a very democratic man, detested the idea of servility in any kind of servant, although he rather liked it in members of the family.

Carl Jonas

Frank Harris told the truth, according to Max Beerbohm, only "when his invention flagged."

Vincent Brome

Disinterested as the being who made him.

Thomas Jefferson
(speaking of John Adams)

He has peculiar powers as an assailant, and almost always, even when attacked, gets himself into that attitude, by making war upon his accuser; and he has, withal, an instinct for the jugular and the carotid artery, as unerring as that of any carnivorous animal.

Rufus Choate
(*speaking of John Quincy Adams*)

He had a face like a benediction.

Miguel de Cervantes

He was thoroughly American, had never crossed the sea, had never been spoiled by English insularity or French dissipation; a quiet, native, aboriginal man, as an acorn from the oak; no aping of foreigners, no frivolous accomplishments, Kentuckian born, working on a farm, a flatboatman, a captain in the Black Hawk War, a country lawyer, a representative in the rural legislature of Illinois;—on such modest foundations the broad structure of his frame was laid.

Ralph Waldo Emerson
(*speaking of Abraham Lincoln*)

He rowed to his object with muffled oars.

John Randolph
(*speaking of Martin Van Buren*)

He is a man of splendid abilities, but utterly corrupt. He shines and stinks like rotten mackerel by moonlight.

John Randolph
(speaking of Edward Livingston)

Mr. Jefferson came into Congress in June, 1775, and brought with him a reputation for literature, science, and a happy talent of composition. Writings of his were handed about, remarkable for the peculiar felicity of expression. Though a silent member in Congress, he was so prompt, frank, explicit, and decisive upon committees and in conversation— not even Samuel Adams was more so—that he soon seized upon my heart.

John Adams

Ein Gott-betrunkener Mensch.

A God-intoxicated man.

Novalis (speaking of Spinoza)

. . . one finds no twilight region in his mind, and no capacity for dreaminess or passivity. All parts of it are filled with the same noonday glare, like a dry desert where every grain of sand shows singly, and there are no mysteries or shadows.

William James
(speaking of Herbert Spencer)

There is a piece missing; I have never been able to discover
what it is.
                                          Napoleon Bonaparte
                                  (*speaking of Tsar Alexander I*)

He went on to say, with a smile at his homely metaphor,
that Gertrude's bark was worth more than her bite. This
was foolish—Gertrude's bark *was* her bite; and many a bite
has lain awake all night longing to be Gertrude's bark.
                                            Randall Jarrell

He was always leaning forward, pushing something invisible ahead of him.
                                             James Thurber
                                    (*speaking of Harold Ross*)

What time he can spare from the adornment of his person
he devotes to the neglect of his duties.
                                               Alan Gregg
                        (*an Oxford don describing a colleague*)

"Warren, it's a good thing you weren't born a gal . . . you'd
be in the family way all the time. You can't say 'No.' "
                                     Warren Harding's father
               (*as quoted in Eric Goldman*, Rendezvous with Destiny)

He has occasional flashes of silence, that make his conversation perfectly delightful.

Sydney Smith
(speaking of Thomas Macaulay)

He has spent all his life in letting down empty buckets into empty wells; and he's frittering away his age in trying to draw them up again.

Sydney Smith
(speaking of a friend)

He is the only diplomat in all history who can strut sitting down.

Hugh Gibson
(comment concerning an unnamed colleague)

He was so generally civil that nobody thanked him for it.

Samuel Johnson

The novelist was in his late forties, tall, reddish, and looked as if life had given him an endless stream of two-timing girl friends, five-day drunks and cars with bad transmissions.

Richard Brautigan

He was just another fellow, made in God's image and wearing a white shirt with a ready-tied black bow tie and jean pants held up with web galluses. Town from the waist up, country from the waist down. Get both votes.

Robert Penn Warren
(*describing Willie in* All the King's Men)

A mighty good sausage-stuffer was spoiled when the man became a poet. He would look well standing under a descending pile driver.

Eugene Field

A solemn, unsmiling, sanctimonious old iceberg that looked like he was waiting for a vacancy in the Trinity.

Mark Twain

He has outsoared the shadow of our night.
Envy and calumny and hate and pain
And that unrest which men miscall delight
Can touch him not and torture not again.

Percy Bysshe Shelley
(*referring to John Keats*)

He has a god in him, though I don't know which god.

Ezra Pound

Gnawed within and scorched without, with the infixed, un-relenting fangs of some incurable idea.

Herman Melville
(*of Ahab in* Moby Dick)

There is a wisdom that is woe; but there is a woe that is madness. And there is a Catskill eagle in some souls that can alike dive down into the blackest gorges, and soar out of them again and become invisible in the sunny spaces.

Herman Melville

> That jewell'd mass of millinery,
> That oil'd and curl'd Assyrian Bull.

Alfred, Lord Tennyson

Buckingham [speaking of the Cardinal of York]:
The devil speed him! no man's pie is freed
From his ambitious finger.

William Shakespeare

Brutus [of Julius Caesar]:
Fashion it thus; that what he is, augmented,
Would run to these and these extremities:
And therefore think him as a serpent's egg

Which hatch'd would as his kind grow mischievous,
And kill him in the shell.
                              William Shakespeare

Malcolm [of Macbeth]: I grant him bloody,
Luxurious, avaricious, false, deceitful,
Sudden, malicious, smacking of every sin
That has a name.
                              William Shakespeare

He is winding up the watch of his wit;
By and by it will strike.
                              William Shakespeare

Malcolm: . . . nothing in his life
Became him like the leaving it; he died
As one that had been studied in his death,
To throw away the dearest thing he owed
As 'twere a careless trifle.
                              William Shakespeare

Honey in his mouth, knives in his heart.
                              Chinese proverb

He has too many lice to feel an itch.

Chinese proverb

Nature made him and then broke the mould.

Ariosto

TWO

Self-Portraits

"Here Are These Two Unaccountable Freaks"

I have endured a great deal of ridicule without much malice, and have received a great deal of kindness not quite free from ridicule.

Abraham Lincoln

Say I'm a philosopher, say I'm a seeker for truth, say I'm a lover of my kind; or, best of all, just say I'm a Student.

Henry James, Sr.

I had an immense advantage over many others dealing with the problem inasmuch as I had no fixed ideas derived from long-established practice to control and bias my mind, and did not suffer from the general belief that whatever is, is right.

Henry Bessemer
(discoverer of new method of producing steel)

I do not know what I may appear to the world, but to myself I seem to have been only like a boy playing on the seashore, and diverting myself in now and then finding a smoother pebble or a prettier shell than ordinary, whilst the great ocean of truth lay all undiscovered before me.

Isaac Newton

I may have my faults, but being wrong ain't one of them.

James Riddle Hoffa

I came in with Halley's Comet in 1835. It is coming again next year, and I expect to go out with it. It will be the greatest disappointment of my life if I don't go out with Halley's Comet. The Almighty has said, no doubt: "Now here are these two unaccountable freaks; they came in together, they must go out together."

Mark Twain
(He was born November 30, 1835, and died April 21, 1910.
Perihelion for Halley's Comet in 1835 was November 16,
and in 1910 was April 20.)

When I was younger I could remember anything, whether it had happened or not.

Mark Twain

When I am right, I get angry. Churchill gets angry when he is wrong. So we were very often angry at each other.

Charles de Gaulle

I have suffered from being misunderstood, but I would have suffered a hell of a lot more if I had been understood.

Clarence Darrow

I am a sick man. . . . I am a spiteful man. I am an unattractive man. I believe my liver is diseased.

Fyodor Dostoevsky
(*narrator in* Notes from Underground)

I got a simple rule about everybody. If you don't treat me right—shame on you!

Louis Armstrong

A cowardly act! What do I care about that? You may be sure that I should never fear to commit one if it were to my advantage.

Napoleon Bonaparte

(In a letter to his grandmother at the age of eight): I will give you a description of my occupations. On waking I lift my heart to God. At seven I get up and breakfast happily on fruit. I then translate a little theme from French into Latin; I learn my lessons; I play some piece on the harpsichord; I read Roman History and Homer, which I enjoy very much, especially Homer, because he is a writer whose poetry I love and who amuses me while giving me great ideas.

(A little over a year later, at the age of ten, in a letter to the same grandmother): In spite of what the ancients have thought, I shall not live with them, and I believe I shall drop them while I am at an age to enjoy life with the living. I sometimes see a young English girl here of about

my own age whom I much prefer to Cicero, Seneca, and
the others. . . .

Benjamin Constant

Doolittle: I'm one of the undeserving poor: thats what I
am. Think of what that means to a man. It means that hes
up agen middle class morality all the time. If theres anything going, and I put in for a bit of it, it's always the
same story: "Youre undeserving; so you can't have it." But
my needs is as great as the most deserving widow that ever
got money out of six different charities in one week for the
death of the same husband. I dont need less than a deserving
man: I need more. I dont eat less hearty than him; and I
drink a lot more. I want a bit of amusement, cause I'm a
thinking man. I want cheerfulness and a song and a band
when I feel low. Well, they charge me just the same for
everything as they charge the deserving. What is middle
class morality? Just an excuse for never giving me anything.
Therefore, I ask you, as two gentlemen, not to play that
game on me. I'm playing straight with you. I aint pre-
tending to be deserving. I'm undeserving; and I mean to go
on being undeserving. I like it; and thats the truth.

George Bernard Shaw

Thomas: I have left
Rings of beer on every alehouse table
From the salt sea-coast across half a dozen countries
But each time I thought I was on the way

To a faintly festive hiccup
The sight of the damned world sobered me up again.

Christopher Fry

Wolsey: (when his duplicity is discovered):
                    Nay then, farewell!
I have touched the highest point of all my greatness;
And, from that full meridian of my glory,
I haste now to my setting: I shall fall
Like a bright exhalation in the evening,
And no man see me more.

William Shakespeare

THREE

Life and the Living

"Life Is a Predicament"

∾ ∾ ∾

Life is not a spectacle or a feast; it is a predicament.

George Santayana

For everything that lives is holy, life delights in life.

William Blake

This only is certain, that there is nothing certain, and nothing more miserable and yet more arrogant than man.

Pliny

Life cannot wait until the sciences may have explained the universe scientifically. We cannot put off living until we are ready. The most salient characteristic of life is its coerciveness: it is always urgent, "here and now" without any possible postponement. Life is fired at us point blank.

Jose Ortega y Gasset

My opinion of mankind as a brilliant success needs a good deal of nursing.

H. W. Shaw

My respect for individuals is a respect for their right to be, to live, to explore their own potentialities, to find their own salvation, to achieve what dignity they can. It is not an in-discriminate enthusiasm for the general level of human per-formance. Great talent and the high virtues are thinly dis-persed and no intensity of democratic sentiment will change that fact.

D. Sutten

Man is the missing link between the ape and the human being.

Author unknown

Men fade like the leaves. They are emblems of imbecility, images of clay, a race lightsome and without substance, creatures of a day, without wings.

Aristophanes

If *this* be the whole fruit of the victory, we say; if the generations of mankind suffered and laid down their lives; if prophets confessed and martyrs sang in the fire, and all the sacred tears were shed for no other end than that a race of creatures of such unexampled insipidity should succeed, and protract *in saecula saeculorum* their contented and in-offensive lives—why, at such a rate, better lose than win the battle, or at all events better ring down the curtain before the last act of the play, so that a business that began so im-portantly may be saved from so singularly flat a winding-up.

William James

Presumption is our natural and original infirmity. The frailest and most vulnerable of all creatures is man, and at the same time the most arrogant.

Montaigne

Numberless are the world's wonders, but none
More wonderful than man . . .
. . . from every wind
He has made himself secure—from all but one:
In the late wind of death he cannot stand.

Sophocles

Existence is no more than a flaw in the perfection of non-existence.

Paul Valéry

The idea of disdaining life is ridiculous. For after all it is our being, it is our all. The things that have a richer and a nobler being may condemn ours. But it is contrary to Nature that we should despise and carelessly set ourselves at naught. It is a malady confined to man, and not seen in any other creature, to hate and despise himself. It is on a par with our vanity to desire to be other than we are. We reap no fruit from such a desire, seeing that it contradicts and hinders itself.

Montaigne

For if there is a sin against life, it consists perhaps not so much in despairing of life as in hoping for another life and in eluding the implacable grandeur of this life.

Albert Camus

Reason thus with life:
If I do lose thee, I do lose a thing
That none but fools would keep.

William Shakespeare

Life is barren enough surely with all her trappings; let us therefore be cautious how we strip her.

Samuel Johnson

I feel no need for any other faith than my faith in human beings. Like Confucius of old, I am so absorbed in the wonder of the earth, and the life upon it that I cannot think of heaven and the angels.

Pearl Buck

To live is like to love—all reason is against it, and all healthy instinct for it.

Samuel Butler

Man is the only animal that laughs and weeps; for he is the only animal that is struck with the difference between what things are, and what they ought to be.

William Hazlitt

The world is a comedy to those who think and a tragedy to those who feel.

Horace Walpole

A touch of folly is needed if we are to extricate ourselves successfully from some of the hazards of life.

La Rochefoucauld

The diseases which destroy a man are no less natural than the instincts which preserve him.

George Santayana

Life is an error-making and an error-correcting process, and nature in marking man's papers will grade him for wisdom as measured both by survival and by the quality of life of those who survive.

Jonas Salk

The measure of a happy Life is not from the fewer or more Suns we behold, the fewer or more Breaths we draw . . . but from the having once lived well, acted our Part handsomely, and made our Exit cheerfully, and as became us.

Shaftesbury

Nothing will repay a man for becoming inhuman. The aim of life is some way of living, as flexible and gentle as human nature; so that ambition may stoop to kindness, and philosophy to candor and humor. Neither prosperity nor empire nor heaven can be worth winning at the price of a virulent temper, bloody hands, an anguished spirit, and a vain hatred of the rest of the world.

George Santayana

Nothing can be meaner than the anxiety to live on, to live on anyhow and in any shape; a spirit with any honour is not willing to live except in its own way, and a spirit with any wisdom is not overeager to live at all.

George Santayana

. . . his personal idea was one of the human being conditioned by other human beings, and knowing that present arrangements were not, *sub specie aeternitatis, the* truth, but that one should be satisfied with such truth as one could get by approximation. Trying to live with a civil heart.

With disinterested charity. With a sense of the mystic potency of humankind. With an inclination to believe in archetypes of goodness. A desire for virtue was no accident.

Saul Bellow

Some go through life getting free rides; others pay full fare and something extra to take care of the free riders. Some of the free riders are those who make an art of "knowing the angles," others are rascals, others lazy; but some really need help and could not ride unless they rode free. I don't spend much time worrying about the free riders; but I am a full-fare man, first and last.

D. Sutten

Stulti timent fortunam, sapientes ferunt.

The stupid fear fortune, the wise endure it.

Latin proverb

Life is the art of drawing sufficient conclusions from insufficient premises.

Samuel Butler

No man deals out his money to others; every man deals out his time and his life. Of nothing are we so prodigal as of those things in which alone avarice would be useful and commendable.

Montaigne

. . . life must be understood backwards. But . . . it must be lived forwards.

Sören Kierkegaard

To consider the world in its length and breadth, its various history, the many races of man, their starts, their fortunes, their mutual alienation, their conflicts; and then their ways, habits, governments, forms of worship; their enterprises, their aimless courses, their random achievements. . . . the tokens so faint and broken of a superintending design, the blind evolution of what turn out to be great powers and truths, the progress of things, as if from unreasoning elements, not toward final causes, the greatness and littleness of man, his far-reaching aims, his short duration, the curtain hung over his futurity . . . the defeat of good, the success of evil . . . the pervading idolatries, the corruptions . . . all this is a vision to dizzy and appall; and inflicts upon the mind the sense of profound mystery, which is absolutely beyond solution. What shall be said to this heart-piercing, reason-bewildering fact?

Cardinal Newman

FOUR

The Life Cycle

"Life Is an Onion and One Peels It Crying"

Life is an onion and one peels it crying.

French proverb

Actually, the process of birth continues. The child begins to recognize outside objects, to react affectively, to grasp things and to co-ordinate his movements, to walk. But birth continues. The child learns to speak, it learns to know the use and function of things, it learns to relate itself to others, to avoid punishment and gain praise and liking. Slowly, the growing person learns to love, to develop reason, to look at the world objectively. He begins to develop his powers; to acquire a sense of identity, to overcome the seduction of his senses for the sake of an integrated life. . . . The whole life of the individual is nothing but the process of giving birth to himself; indeed, we should be fully born, when we die— although it is the tragic fate of most individuals to die before they are born.

Erich Fromm

We are born crying, live complaining, and die disappointed.

Thomas Fuller

Each day is a little life; every waking and rising a little birth, every fresh morning a little youth, every going to rest and sleep a little death.

Arthur Schopenhauer

The utmost span of a man's life is a hundred years. Half of it is spent in night, and of the rest half is lost by childhood and old age. Work, grief, longing and illness make up what remains.

Bhartrihari

Nascentes morimur, finisque ab origine pendet.

We start to die when we are born, and the end depends on the beginning.

Latin proverb

Los árboles en el monte tienen
    su separación.
Unos nacen para santos y otros
    par ser carbon.
The trees that grow on the mountain
All go their separate ways.
Some are born to be carved into saints,
Some as charcoal end their days.

Spanish rhyme

Madre que consiente, engorda una serpiente.

The mother who spoils her child, fattens a serpent.

Spanish proverb

Carlyle, son of a mason and grandson of a carpenter, showed his gifts early. At the age of eleven months he heard another child in the household crying and although he had never, before that, uttered a word he sat up and said "What ails wee Jock?"

Catherine M. Cox

It's not easy to be crafty and winsome at the same time, and few accomplish it after the age of six.

D. Sutten

(When Bulwer-Lytton was eight years old, he did some reading in metaphysics and presumably under the influence of this reading he one day inquired of his mother): "Pray, Mama, are you not sometimes overcome by the sense of your identity?" (It was this remark that determined his mother to place him in school.)

Catherine M. Cox

When a boy is eleven years old you had better find something to engage his interest. I offer it as a theorem that a boy that age is either doing something or breaking something.

Jerrold R. Zacharias

My object will be, if possible, to form Christian men, for Christian boys I can scarcely hope to make.

Thomas Arnold
(on appointment to headmastership of Rugby)

A child can combat cruelty, but overbearing kindness buys his subjection in a currency he has not learned to reject. If he accepts, he is enslaved; if he escapes, guilt-ridden.

D. Sutten

If you refuse to be made straight when you are green, you will not be made straight when you are dry.

African proverb

The angry and reverent spirit characteristic of youth seems to find no peace until it has falsified men and things in such a way that it can vent its passion against them.

Friedrich Nietzsche

There's nothing wrong with teenagers that reasoning with them won't aggravate.

Author unknown

When I was a boy of fourteen, my father was so ignorant I could hardly stand to have the old man around. But when I got to be twenty-one, I was astonished at how much the old man had learned in seven years.

Mark Twain

The more you love your children the more care you should take to neglect them occasionally. The web of affection can be drawn too tight.

D. Sutten

There is a time somewhere between early adolescence and job-hunting—when a young man is ripe for a certain solitude; when he can hear things he could not hear before, and will be deaf to later; when he can make those combinations of thought and feeling that he will one day sternly separate into "reason" and "emotion," each in its lonely grave.

Harry C. McPherson

A young Trooper should have an old Horse.

Thomas Fuller

I hate the young. . . . Give me some good old rain-soaked clubman who can't be improved.

John Jay Chapman

Maturity: among other things, not to hide one's strength
out of fear and, consequently, live below one's best.

Dag Hammarskjöld

How many "coming men" has one known! Where on earth
do they all go to?

Arthur Pinero

The maturity of man—to have reacquired the seriousness he
had as a child at play.

Friedrich Nietzsche

Maturity is a bitter disappointment for which no remedy
exists, . . . unless laughter can be said to remedy anything.

Kurt Vonnegut, Jr.

You are looking for a rich husband. At your age I looked
for hardship, danger, horror and death, that I might feel the
life in me more intensely. I did not let the fear of death
govern my life; and my reward was, I had my life. You are
going to let the fear of poverty govern your life and your
reward will be that you will eat, but you will not live.

George Bernard Shaw

The procreation of mankind is a great marvel and mystery. Had God consulted me in the matter, I should have advised him to continue the generation of the species by fashioning them of clay, in the way Adam was fashioned.

Martin Luther

Nothing has a stronger influence psychologically on their environment, and especially on their children, than the un-lived life of the parents.

C. G. Jung

Si tu mujer te dice que te tires por un tajo, ruégale a Dios que sea bajo.

If your wife tells you to throw yourself off a cliff, pray to God that it be a low one.

Spanish proverb

There comes a time when rebellious young people should take their turn as adults against whom the next wave of youngsters can rebel.

D. Sutten

If you persist to the threshold of old age—your fiftieth year, let us say—you will be a powerful person yourself, with an accretion of peculiarities which other people will have to study in order to square you. The toes you will have trodden on by this time will be as the sands on the seashore; and from far below you will mount the roar of a ruthless multitude of young men in a hurry. You may perhaps grow to be aware what they are in a hurry to do. They are in a hurry to get you out of the way.

F. M. Cornford

Old birds are hard to pluck.

German proverb

The man who sees two or three generations is like one who sits in the conjuror's booth at a fair, and sees the tricks two or three times. They are meant to be seen only once.

Arthur Schopenhauer

I know not whether increasing years do not cause us to esteem fewer people and to bear with more.

Shenstone

Orinthia. . . . Live a really noble and beautiful life—a kingly life—with me. What ¿ ou need to make you a real king is a real queen.

Magnus. But I have got one.

Orinthia. Oh, you are blind. You are worse than blind; you have low tastes. Heaven is offering you a rose; and you cling to a cabbage.

Magnus. (Laughing) That is a very apt metaphor, beloved. But what wise man, if you force him to choose between doing without roses and doing without cabbages, would not secure the cabbages? Besides, all these old married cabbages were once roses; and, though young things like you don't remember that, their husbands do.

George Bernard Shaw

It is the privilege of adults to give advice. It is the privilege of youth not to listen. Both avail themselves of their privileges, and the world rocks along.

D. Sutten

The young man knows the rules but the old man knows the exceptions.

Dr. Oliver Wendell Holmes

In spite of everything, I am convinced that in other times Marshal Pétain would not have consented to don the purple in the midst of national surrender. . . . But alas! under the outer shell, the years had gnawed his character. Age was delivering him over to the maneuvers of people who were clever at covering themselves with his majestic lassitude. Old age is a shipwreck.

Charles de Gaulle
(on Pétain's collaboration with the Germans
after the fall of France in 1940)

There are people whose watch stops at a certain hour and who remain permanently at that age.

Sainte-Beuve

When you win, you're an old pro. When you lose you're an old man.

Charlie Conerly
(of the New York Giants)

Once I had the strength but no wisdom; now I have the wisdom but no strength.

Persian proverb

Our judgment ripens; our imagination decays. We cannot at once enjoy the flowers of the Spring of life and the fruits of its Autumn.

Thomas Macaulay

The long habit of living indisposeth us for dying.

Thomas Browne

Death keeps no calendar.

Thomas Fuller

Some men are more missed than lamented, when they die; others are deeply mourned but scarcely missed.

La Rochefoucauld

If this is dying, I don't think much of it.

Lytton Strachey
(*on his deathbed*)

It is good to die before one has done anything deserving death.

Anaxandrides

Gegen den Tod ist kein Kraut gewachsen.
For death there is no medicine.

German proverb

By my troth, I care not, a man can die but once:
We owe God a death . . .

William Shakespeare

When thou dost hear a toll or knell
Then think upon thy passing bell.
                                    John Ray

Farewell, a long farewell, to all my greatness!
This is the state of man: today he puts forth
The tender leaves of hope; tomorrow blossoms,
And bears his blushing honors thick upon him:
The third day comes a frost, a killing frost,
And when he thinks, good easy man, full surely
His greatness is a-ripening, nips his root,
And then he falls, as I do.
                        William Shakespeare
                        (*Wolsey in* Henry VIII)

What is the world to a man when his wife is a widow.
                                    Irish proverb

Why dost thou fear thy last day? It contributes no more
to thy death than does every other day. The last step does
not cause the lassitude: it declares it. All days journey towards death; the last arrives there.
                                    Montaigne

Praise day at night, and life at the end.
                                    George Herbert

FIVE

Life Activity

"Better Than Loafing Around Hades"

∽ ∽ ∽

It was not the futility, but the monotony, of Sisyphus' task that made it a punishment to keep rolling the stone up the mountain, only to have it fall down again. If he could have picked different stones, or different mountains, or even different ways of pushing the same stone up the same mountain, he might very well have counted it a reward. Certainly this would have been better than just loafing around Hades.

Charles Curtis

The best part of one's life is the working part, the creative part. Believe me, I love to succeed. . . . However, the real spiritual and emotional excitement is in the doing.

Garson Kanin

If the world were merely seductive, that would be easy. If it were merely challenging, that would be no problem. But I arise in the morning torn between a desire to improve (or save) the world and a desire to enjoy (or savor) the world. This makes it hard to plan the day.

E. B. White

Nothing is worth doing unless the consequences may be serious.

George Bernard Shaw

We do what we must, and call it by the best names we can, and would fain have the praise of having intended the result which ensues.

Ralph Waldo Emerson

Business is really more agreeable than pleasure; it interests the whole mind, the aggregate nature of man more continuously, and more deeply. But it does not *look* as if it did.

Walter Bagehot

The excitement of the chase is properly our quarry. We are not to be pardoned if we carry it on badly or foolishly; to fail to seize the prey is a different matter. For we are born to search after the truth; to possess it belongs to a greater power.

The world is but a school of research. The question is not who shall hit the ring, but who shall run the best course.

Montaigne

Yet all men of goodwill have this in common—that our works in the end put us to shame; that always we must begin them afresh, and our sacrifice be eternally renewed.

Hermann Hesse

Pursue, keep up with, circle round and round your life, as a dog does his master's chaise. Do what you love. Know

your own bone; gnaw at it, bury it, unearth it, and gnaw it
still.

Henry David Thoreau

Do you not know that disease and death must needs over-
take us, no matter what we are doing? . . . What do you
wish to be doing when it overtakes you? . . . If you have
anything better to be doing when you are so overtaken, get
to work on that.

Epictetus

My heart bids me do it, if I can, and it is a thing possible
to do.

Homer

The heart to conceive, the understanding to direct, and the
hand to execute.

Junius

Let me tell you the secret that has led me to my goal. My
strength lies solely in my tenacity.

Louis Pasteur

Gnaw the bone which is fallen to thy lot.

Ben Syra

I confess that altruistic and cynically selfish talk seem to me about equally unreal. With all humility, I think "Whatsoever thy hand findeth to do, do it with thy might" infinitely more important than the vain attempt to love one's neighbor as one's self. If you want to hit a bird on the wing you must have all your will in focus, you must not be thinking about yourself, and equally, you must not be thinking about your neighbor; you must be living in your eye on that bird. Every achievement is a bird on the wing.

Oliver Wendell Holmes, Jr.

Brother, I have watched men: their insect cares and giant projects—their godlike plans and their mouselike employments—their eager race after happiness . . . this checkered lottery of life, on which so many stake their innocence and Heaven to snatch a prize, and—blanks are all they draw; for they find to their disappointment that there was no prize in the wheel.

J. C. F. Schiller

Come let us mock at the great
That had such burdens on the mind
And toiled so hard and late
To leave some monument behind
Nor thought of the leveling wind.

William Butler Yeats

The race is not to the swift, nor the battle to the strong, neither yet bread to the wise, nor yet riches to men of un-

derstanding, nor yet favor to men of skill; but time and
chance happeneth to them all.

Ecclesiastes 9:11

Life is at best only a children's game.
Yet the game must be played conscientiously.

Fukuzawa Yukichi

God gives the nuts, but he does not crack them.

German proverb

If this life be not a real fight, in which something is eternally gained for the universe by success, it is no better than
a game of private theatricals from which one may with-
draw at will. But it feels like a real fight—as if there were
something really wild in the universe which we, with all
our idealities and faithfulnesses, are needed to redeem.

William James

Existence is a strange bargain. Life owes us little; we owe it
everything. The only true happiness comes from squander-
ing ourselves for a purpose.

John Mason Brown

This is the true joy in life, the being used for a purpose
recognized by yourself as a mighty one; the being thor-

oughly worn out before you are thrown on the scrap heap; the being a force of Nature instead of a feverish, selfish little clod of ailments and grievances complaining that the world will not devote itself to making you happy.

George Bernard Shaw

Do not seek to follow in the footsteps of the men of old; seek what they sought.

Matsuo Basho

Never take a course of action on the sole grounds that reprehensible people are urging the opposite course.

D. Sutten

The youth gets together his materials to build a bridge to the moon, or perchance a palace or temple on the earth, and at length the middleaged man concludes to build a wood-shed with them.

Henry David Thoreau

O my soul, do not aspire to immortal life, but exhaust the limits of the possible.

Pindar

Nothing is ours outright, as a gift; we have to perform for ourselves even those of our actions which seem most passive. The humble Sancho Panza kept suggesting this on all occasions, by repeating his proverb: "If they give you the cow, you have to carry the rope." All we are given is possibilities—to make ourselves one thing or another.

Jose Ortega y Gasset

We who lived in concentration camps can remember the men who walked through the huts comforting others, giving away their last piece of bread. They may have been few in number, but they offer sufficient proof that everything can be taken from a man but one thing: the last of the human freedoms—to choose one's attitude in any given set of circumstances, to choose one's own way.

Victor Frankl

. . . many have but one resource to sustain them in their misery, and that is to think, "Circumstances have been against me. . . . I have never had a great love . . . but that is because I have never met a man or a woman . . . worthy of it; if I have not written . . . good books, it is because I had not the leisure." . . . But . . . for the existentialist, there is no love apart from deeds of love; no potentiality of love other than that which is manifested in loving; there is no genius other than that which is expressed in works of art.

Jean Paul Sartre

I dread success. To have succeeded is to have finished one's business on earth, like the male spider, who is killed by the female the moment he has succeeded in his courtship. I like a state of continual becoming, with a goal in front and not behind.

George Bernard Shaw

The riders in a race do not stop short when they reach the goal. There is a little finishing canter before coming to a standstill. There is time to hear the kind voice of friends and to say to one's self: "The work is done." But just as one says that, the answer comes: "The race is over, but the work never is done while the power to work remains." The canter that brings you to a standstill need not be only coming to rest. It cannot be while you still live. For to live is to function. That is all there is in living. And so I end with a line from a Latin poet who uttered the message more than fifteen hundred years ago. "Death plucks my ears and says, Live—I am coming."

Oliver Wendell Holmes, Jr.
(Radio address on his ninetieth birthday)

What fools we are! "He has spent his life in idleness," we say; "I have done nothing today." What, have you not lived? That is not only the fundamental but the most honorable of your occupations. "If I had been given an opportunity to manage great affairs, I might have shown what I can do." Have you been able to meditate and manage your own life? Then you have performed the greatest work of all. . . .

It is our duty to compose our character, not to compose books and to win, not battles and provinces, but order and tranquility for our conduct of life.

Our great and glorious masterpiece is to live to the purpose.

Montaigne

I must be used, built into the solid fabric of your life as far as there is any usable brick in me, and thrown aside when I am used up. It is only when I am being used that I can feel my own existence, enjoy my own life.

George Bernard Shaw

Our chief want in life is somebody who will make us do what we can.

Ralph Waldo Emerson

I am satisfied there is nothing to be done but to make the best of what cannot be helped, to act with reason oneself and with a good conscience. And though that will not give all the joys some people wish for, yet it will make one very quiet.

Sarah, Duchess of Marlborough

We act as though it were our mission to bring about the triumph of truth, but our mission is only to fight for it.

Blaise Pascal

It is the privilege of any human work which is well done to invest the doer with a certain haughtiness. He can well afford not to conciliate, whose faithful work will answer for him.

Ralph Waldo Emerson

. . . there are those . . . who see themselves as a word to be communicated, an indignation to be vented, or a charitable act that must be done. They . . . suffer sharply . . . until they have delivered themselves of the word, the wrath, or the kindness that is their reason for being.

Jose Marti

There is a well-worn adage that those who set out upon a great enterprise would do well to count the cost. I am not sure that this is always true. I think that some of the very greatest enterprises in this world have been carried out successfully simply because the people who undertook them did not count the cost; and I am much of the opinion that, in this very case, the most instructive consideration for us is the cost of doing nothing.

Thomas Henry Huxley

No noble thing can be done without risks.
Montaigne

Individuality is something to be built for the sake of something else. It is a structure of potential energies for expenditure in the service of an idea, a cultural endeavor, the betterment of man, an emergent value. I am proposing that an individual self is made only to be lost—that is, only to pledge itself to some enterprise that is in league with a good future; and thereby find itself once more; but this time as the actor of a living myth, an instrument of culture.
Henry A. Murray

To which may be added that other Aristotelian consideration, that the man who benefits another loves him better than he is loved by the other; and that he to whom a thing is owing loves better than he who owes. Every artisan loves his work better than he would be loved by the work if it had feeling; since Being is a thing to be cherished, and Being consists in motion and action. Wherefore every one in some sort lives in his work. He who benefits another does a beautiful and worthy deed; he who receives, only a useful one.
Montaigne

Every calling is great when greatly pursued.
Oliver Wendell Holmes, Jr.

With the ant-heap the respectable race of ants began and with the ant-heap they will probably end, which does the greatest credit to their perseverance and good sense. But man is a frivolous and incongruous creature, and perhaps, like a chess player, loves the process of the game, not the end of it. And who knows (there is no saying with certainty), perhaps the only goal on earth to which mankind is striving lies in this incessant process of attaining, in other words, in life itself, and not in the thing to be attained, which must always be expressed as a formula, as positive as twice two makes four, and such positiveness is not life, gentlemen, but is the beginning of death.

Fyodor Dostoevsky

SIX

Thought

"No Defense Except Stupidity"

There is no defense, except stupidity, against the impact of a new idea.

P. W. Bridgman

Man is but a reed, the most feeble thing in nature, but he is a thinking reed.

Blaise Pascal

If a little knowledge is dangerous, where is the man who knows so much as to be out of danger.

Thomas Henry Huxley

It seems as though I had not drunk from the cup of wisdom, but had fallen into it.

Sören Kierkegaard

Tiresias (to Oedipus):
How dreadful knowledge of the truth can be when there's no help in truth!

Sophocles

He, O men, is wisest of you all who has learned, like Socrates, that his wisdom is worth nothing.

Plato

"A philosopher," said the theologian, "is like a blind man in a darkened room looking for a black cat that isn't there." "That is right," the philosopher replied, "and if he were a theologian, he'd find it."

Anonymous

I have always instinctively dreaded mysticism (although fascinated by it) as endangering the light of reason—a poor light, nearly always smoking, and often stinking, but yet all we have to let us go forward a few feet in a century toward a positive, materially better world, opening out greater possibilities of genuine and not merely ecstatically illusive states of euphoria.

Bernard Berenson

A good question is never answered. It is not a bolt to be tightened into place but a seed to be planted and to bear more seed toward the hope of greening the landscape of idea. The difference between a seed and an inert speck can be hard to see, but only one of them will grow and return itself in kind and be multiplied.

John Ciardi

Some things I have said of which I am not altogether con-
fident. But that we shall be better and braver and less help-
less if we think we ought to inquire than we should have
been if we had indulged in the idle fancy that there was no
knowing and no use seeking to know what we do not
know—that is a theme on which I am ready to fight, in
word and deed, to the utmost of my power.

Plato (Socrates in the Meno)

The Greeks possessed a knowledge of mankind which we
apparently can hardly attain without going through the
invigorating hibernation of a new barbarism.

George C. Lichtenberg

Listen to the sad story of mankind, who like children lived
until I gave them understanding and a portion of reason.

Aeschylus

Wisdom consists in rising superior both to madness and to
common sense, and in lending oneself to the universal delu-
sion without becoming its dupe.

Amiel

Folly is our constant companion throughout life. If someone appears wise, it is only because his follies are suited to
his age and station.

La Rochefoucauld

[The] answer was good that Diogenes made to one that asked him in mockery, "How came it to pass that philosophers were the followers of rich men, and not rich men of philosophers?" He answered soberly, and yet sharply, "Because the one sort knew what they have need of, and the other did not."

Francis Bacon

Philosophers are capable of almost endless enjoyment of mutual misunderstanding.

Lyman Bryson

It requires a very unusual mind to undertake the analysis of the obvious.

Alfred North Whitehead

Look at all the sentences which seem true and question them.

David Riesman

Only the hand that erases can write the true thing.

Meister Eckhart

Science has promised us truth—an understanding of such relationships as our minds can grasp; it has never promised us either peace or happiness.

Gustav LeBon

Man has mounted science, and is now run away with. I firmly believe that before many centuries more, science will be the master of man. The engines he will have invented will be beyond his strength to control. Some day science may have the existence of mankind in its power, and the human race may commit suicide by blowing up the world.

Henry Adams (1862)

Every man has a right to utter what he thinks truth, and every other man has a right to knock him down for it.

Samuel Johnson

Singularity in the right hath ruined many; happy those who are convinced of the general opinion.

Benjamin Franklin

Intellectual man had become an explaining creature. . . . The roots of this, the causes of the other, the sources of events, the history, the structure, the reasons why. For the most part, in one ear, out the other. The soul wanted what

it wanted. . . . It sat unhappily on superstructures of ex-
planation, poor bird, not knowing which way to fly.

Saul Bellow

Mankind misses its opportunities, and its failures are a fair
target for ironic criticism. But the fact that reason too often
fails does not give fair ground for the hysterical conclusion
that it never suceeds. Reason can be compared to the force
of gravitation, the weakest of all natural forces, but in the
end the creator of suns and of stellar systems: those great
societies of the Universe.

Alfred North Whitehead

The aim of science is to seek the simplest explanations of
complex facts. We are apt to fall into the error of thinking
that the facts are simple because simplicity is the goal of
our quest. The guiding motto in the life of every natural
philosopher should be, "Seek simplicity and distrust it!"

Alfred North Whitehead

Sit down before fact as a little child, be prepared to give up
every preconceived notion, follow humbly wherever and
to whatever abysses nature leads, or you shall learn nothing.

Thomas Henry Huxley

We put thirty spokes together and call it a wheel;
But it is on the space where there is nothing that the use-
    fulness of the wheel depends.
We turn clay to make a vessel;
But it is on the space where there is nothing that the use-
    fulness of the vessel depends.
We pierce doors and windows to make a house;
And it is on these spaces where there is nothing that the use-
    fulness of the house depends.
Therefore just as we take advantage of what is, we should
    recognize the usefulness of what is not.

Lao-tzu

My studies in Speculative philosophy, metaphysics, and
science are all summed up in the image of a mouse called
man running in and out of every hole in the Cosmos hunt-
ing for the Absolute Cheese.

Benjamin DeCasseres

Everyone is a genius at least once a year. The real geniuses
simply have their bright ideas closer together.

George C. Lichtenberg

The difference between genius and stupidity is that genius
has its limits.

Author unknown

If it's a bad rule, that is no reason for making a bad exception to it.

Oliver Wendell Holmes, Jr.

Naturae enim non imperatur, nisi parendo.

We cannot command nature except by obeying her.

Francis Bacon

It is better to know nothing than to know what ain't so.

H. W. Shaw

The man who fears no truths has nothing to fear from lies.

Thomas Jefferson

Though all the winds of doctrine were let loose to play upon the earth so Truth be in the field we do ingloriously, by licensing and prohibiting, to misdoubt her strength.

John Milton

A man who talks nonsense so well must know that he is talking nonsense.

Samuel Johnson (of Rousseau)

The most exquisite folly is made of wisdom spun too fine.

Benjamin Franklin

I would rather discover a single causal connection than win the throne of Persia.

Democritus

It's foolish to suppose that we can liberate ourselves from the conventional wisdom at no other cost than that of deriding conventional wisdom. History is full of examples of lonely thinkers who were belittled by the established figures of the time and who, it now turns out, were deservedly neglected.

Leon Lipson

When men have realized that time has upset many fighting faiths, they may come to believe even more than they believe the very foundations of their own conduct that the ultimate good desired is better reached by free trade in ideas—that the best test of truth is the power of the thought to get itself accepted in the competition of the market, and that truth is the only ground upon which their wishes safely can be carried out.

Oliver Wendell Holmes, Jr.

The end of man is knowledge but there's one thing he can't know. He can't know whether knowledge will save him or

kill him. He will be killed, all right, but he can't know
whether he is killed because of the knowledge which he
has got or because of the knowledge which he hasn't got
and which if he had it would save him.

Robert Penn Warren

There are many people who reach their conclusions about
life like schoolboys; they cheat their master by copying the
answer out of a book without having worked out the sum
for themselves.

Sören Kierkegaard

A vision of truth which does not call upon us to get out of
our armchair—why, this is the desideratum of mankind.

John Jay Chapman

The wind in a man's face makes him wise.

John Ray

The house of delusions is cheap to build but draughty to
live in, and ready at any instant to fall; and it is surely
truer prudence to move our furniture betimes into the open
air than to stay indoors until our tenement tumbles about

our ears. It is and it must in the long run be better for man to see things as they are than to be ignorant of them.

A. E. Housman

Love truth but pardon error.

Voltaire

Knowledge rests not upon truth alone, but upon error also.

C. G. Jung

Adversity makes men wise but not rich.

John Ray

Not to know is bad; not to wish to know is worse.

African proverb

It is better to be lost than to be saved all alone; and it is wrong to one's kind to wish to be wise without making others share our wisdom. It is, besides, an illusion to suppose that such a privilege is possible, when everything proves the solidarity of individuals, and when no one can think at all except by means of the general store of thought, accumulated and refined by centuries of cultivation and experience. Absolute individualism is an absurdity.

Amiel

There is a moment when individualism becomes a uniform in spite of itself.

Malcolm Cowley

How dieth the wise man? As the fool.

Ecclesiastes 2:16

SEVEN

Education

"Know or Listen to Those Who Know"

≈ ≈ ≈

Saber o escuchar a los que saben.

Know or listen to those who know.

Balthasar Gracian

In all education the main cause of failure is staleness.

Alfred North Whitehead

To those who want salvation cheap, and most men do, there is very little comfort to be had out of the great teachers.

Walter Lippmann

Learning makes a Man fit Company for himself.

Thomas Fuller

Pedants sneer at an education which is useful. But if education is not useful, what is it? . . . Of course, education should be useful, whatever is your aim in life. It was useful to Saint Augustine and it was useful to Napoleon. It is useful, because understanding is useful.

Alfred North Whitehead

Style is the ultimate morality of mind.

Alfred North Whitehead

To understand things we must have been once in them and then have come out of them; so that first there must be captivity and then deliverance, illusion followed by disillusion, enthusiasm by disappointment. He who is still under the spell, and he who has never felt the spell, are equally incompetent. We only know well what we have first believed, then judged. To understand we must be free, yet not have been always free. The same truth holds, whether it is a question of love, of art, of religion, or of patriotism. Sympathy is a first condition of criticism; reason and justice presuppose, at their origin, emotion.

Amiel

I respect faith but doubt is what gets you an education.

Wilson Mizner

Effective knowledge is professionalised knowledge, supported by a restricted acquaintance with useful subjects subservient to it.

This situation has its dangers. It produces minds in a groove. Each profession makes progress, but it is progress in its own groove. Now to be mentally in a groove is to live in contemplating a given set of abstractions. The groove prevents straying across country, and the abstraction abstracts from something to which no further attention is paid. But there is no groove of abstractions which is adequate for the comprehension of human life. Thus in the modern world, the celibacy of the medieval learned class has been replaced by a celibacy of the intellect which is divorced from the concrete contemplation of the complete facts.

Alfred North Whitehead

Absolute detachment is a polar region, unfit for human life; but one might well make an effort to get out of the steaming jungles, and come a bit closer to the pole.

Crane Brinton

I'm all in favor of the democratic principle that one idiot is as good as one genius, but I draw the line when someone takes the next step and concludes that two idiots are better than one genius.

Leo Szilard

The past as embodied in contemporary adults is both the bed of reactionaries and the springboard of innovators. It provides a man's working capital, whether he squanders it, lives on the interest, or invests it in new enterprises. The extent of his education is the extent to which he enters into effective possession of this patrimony, to which all members of the group have the same hereditary title.

Ralph Barton Perry

Education is a companion which no misfortune can depress, no crime can destroy, no enemy can alienate, no despotism can enslave. At home a friend, abroad an introduction, in solitude a solace, and in society an ornament. It chastens vice, it guides virtue, it gives, at once, grace and government to genius. Without it, what is man? A splendid slave, a reasoning savage.

Joseph Addison

Promote then as an object of primary importance, institutions for the general diffusion of knowledge. In proportion as the structure of government gives force to public opinion, it is essential that public opinion should be enlightened.

George Washington

In the conditions of modern life the rule is absolute, the race which does not value trained intelligence is doomed.

Alfred North Whitehead

If a nation expects to be ignorant and free, in a state of civilization, it expects what never was and never will be.

Thomas Jefferson

In the dark ages, very great men often appeared. In those days only a man whom nature had expressly marked for greatness could become great. Now that education is so easy, men are drilled for greatness, just as dogs are trained to retrieve. In this way we've discovered a new sort of genius, those great at being drilled. These are the people who are mainly spoiling the market.

George C. Lichtenberg

Indiscriminate study bloats the mind.

D. Sutten

You have letters but no learning that understand so many languages, turn over so many volumes, and yet are but asleep when all is done.

John Milton

Beware of the man who works hard to learn something, learns it, and finds himself no wiser than before. . . . He is full of murderous resentment of people who are ignorant without having come by their ignorance the hard way.

Kurt Vonnegut, Jr.

You know . . . everybody is ignorant, only on different subjects.

Will Rogers

Education which is not modern shares the fate of all organic things which are kept too long.

Alfred North Whitehead

Ever learning and never able to come to the knowledge of truth.

Timothy 2:7

In training a child to activity of thought, above all things we must beware of what I will call "inert ideas"—that is to say, ideas that are merely received into the mind without being utilised, or tested, or thrown into fresh combinations. . . . Except at rare intervals of intellectual ferment, education in the past has been radically infected with inert ideas.

Alfred North Whitehead

We must remember that the whole problem of intellectual education is controlled by lack of time. If Methuselah was not a well-educated man, it was his own fault or that of his teachers.

Alfred North Whitehead

The man who is too old to learn was probably always too old to learn.

Haskins

Unafraid before the unknown universe; indifferent to the world's disparagements, and uncorrupted by its prizes.

Learned Hand
(*speaking of his former teachers*)

A student should not be taught more than he can think about.

Alfred North Whitehead

The important thing is not so much that every child should be taught, as that every child should be given the wish to learn.

John Lubbock

No man says of another: "I educated him." It would be offensive and would suggest that the victim was only a puppy when first taken in hand. But it is a proud thing to say, "I taught him"—and a wise one not to specify what.

Jacques Barzun

Organization and method mean much, but contagious human characters mean more in a university.

William James

The secret of teaching is to appear to have known all your life what you learned this afternoon.

Author unknown

No man, however conservative, can stand before a class day after day and refrain from saying more than he knows.

Morris Cohen

Have you learn'd lessons only of those who admired you,
    and were tender with you, and stood aside for you?
Have you not learn'd great lessons from those who reject
    you and brace themselves against you? or who treat you
    with contempt, or dispute the passage with you?

Walt Whitman

The factual teachers were the happiest. They were competent men who knew every detail of their subjects. For them teaching was a job in agriculture. Break up the field of the mind by threats of plowing its wild oats under. Plant the seeds of honest fact—declensions, dates, formulas. Reap the crop at examination time, and woe to the boy with an empty basket.

Henry Seidel Canby

The well-crammed youngster is like a siphon bottle. Press the handle and he fizzes in a welcome relief from pressure.

Henry Seidel Canby

My name it is Benjamin Jowett,
   I'm Master of Balliol College;
Whatever is knowledge I know it,
   And what I don't know isn't knowledge.

Author unknown

We guarantee the quality of our product or return the boy.

A. Lawrence Lowell
(president of Harvard)

Four years of Harvard College, if successful, resulted in an autobiographical blank, a mind on which only a watermark had been stamped.

Henry Adams

If the teacher be corrupt, the world will be corrupt.

Persian proverb

Never try to learn more from an experience than there is in it. There are some vivid and painful experiences that have little to teach us.

D. Sutten

Bad times have a scientific value. These are occasions a good learner would not miss.

Ralph Waldo Emerson

Experience is good, if not bought too dear.

John Ray

Experience makes more timid men than it does wise ones.

H. W. Shaw

I do not believe that sheer suffering teaches. If suffering alone taught, all the world would be wise, since everyone suffers. To suffering must be added mourning, understanding, patience, love, openness and the willingness to remain vulnerable.

Anne Morrow Lindbergh

Torments do rather encourage vices than suppress them; they beget not a care of well-doing, which is the work of reason and discipline, but only a care not to be surprised in doing evil.

Montaigne

People become house builders through building houses, harp players through playing the harp. We grow to be just by doing things which are just.

Aristotle

Men are men before they are lawyers, or physicians, or merchants, or manufacturers; and if you make them capable and sensible men, they will make themselves capable and sensible lawyers and physicians.

John Stuart Mill

I care not whether my pupil is intended for the army, the church or the law. Before his parents chose a calling for him, nature called him to be a man. . . . When he leaves me, he will be neither a magistrate, a soldier, nor a priest; he will be a man.

Jean-Jacques Rousseau

Strange how much you've got to know
Before you know how little you know.

Author unknown

EIGHT

Religion

"Every Life Is a Profession of Faith"

~ ~ ~

Every life is a profession of faith, and exercises an inevitable and silent propaganda. As far as lies in its power, it tends to transform the universe and humanity into its own image. Thus we have all a cure of souls. Every man is a centre of perpetual radiation like a luminous body; he is, as it were, a beacon which entices a ship upon the rocks if it does not guide it into port. Every man is a priest, even involuntarily; his conduct is an unspoken sermon, which is for ever preaching to others;—but there are priests of Baal, of Moloch, and of all the false gods. Such is the high importance of example.

Amiel

God gave burdens, also shoulders.

Yiddish proverb

To believe in the Tao is easy; to keep the Tao is difficult.

Chinese proverb

When in trouble one remembers Allah.

African proverb

The most beautiful and most profound emotion we can experience is the sensation of the mystical. It is the dower of all true science. He to whom this emotion is a stranger, who can no longer wonder and stand rapt in awe, is as good as dead. To know that what is impenetrable to us really exists, manifesting itself as the highest wisdom and the most radiant beauty which our dull faculties can comprehend only in their most primitive forms—this knowledge, this feeling is at the center of true religiousness.

Albert Einstein

Both faith and faithlessness have destroyed men.

Hesiod

Heaven is above us yet; there sits a judge that no king can corrupt.

William Shakespeare

At the day of Doom men shall be judged according to their fruits. It will not be said then, Did you believe? but, Were you doers, or talkers only?

John Bunyan

God does not die on the day when we cease to believe in a personal deity, but we die on the day when our lives cease to be illuminated by the steady radiance, renewed daily, of a wonder, the source of which is beyond all reason.

Dag Hammarskjöld

I believe in the incomprehensibility of God.

Honoré Balzac

We believe as much as we can. We would believe every-thing if we could.

William James

If the stars should appear one night in a thousand years, how would men believe and adore.

Ralph Waldo Emerson

My soul can find no staircase to Heaven unless it be through Earth's loveliness.

Michelangelo

Experience has repeatedly confirmed that well-known maxim of Bacon's, that "a little philosophy inclineth man's mind to atheism, but depth in philosophy bringeth men's minds about to religion."

At the same time, when Bacon penned the sage epigram . . . he forgot to add that the God to whom depth in philosophy brings back men's minds is far from being the same from whom a little philosophy estranges them.

George Santayana

Men of sense are really all of one religion. But men of sense never tell what it is.

Shaftesbury

Fe que no duda es fe muerta.

Faith which does not doubt is a dead faith.

Miguel de Unamuno

Certainly, Nature is unjust and shameless, without probity, and without faith. . . . It is useless to accuse a blind force.

The human conscience, however, revolts against this law of nature, and to satisfy its own instinct of justice it has imagined two hypotheses, out of which it has made for itself a religion,—the idea of an individual providence, and the hypothesis of another life.

In these we have a protest against nature, which is thus declared immoral and scandalous to the moral sense. Man believes in good, and that he may ground himself on justice he maintains that the injustice all around him is but an appearance, a mystery, a cheat, and that justice *will* be done. *Fiat justitia, pereat mundus!*

It is a great act of faith. And since humanity has not made itself, this protest has some chance of expressing a truth. If there is conflict between the natural world and the moral world, between reality and conscience, conscience must be right.

Amiel

One necessary experience on the path to a mature felicity
is full acknowledgment of our utter and unutterable depen-
dence upon Nature, within us and without, the Sun, the
Earth and all that it contains, and upon each other. Acknowledgment of this in one's very marrow gives rise to
that cluster of feelings—wonder, awe, reverence, gratitude,
prayerfulness, and hope—which constitute the passion-center
of religion, the passion-center, I would say, of the best lives
in their profounder workings. Here the myth of individuality
is a hindrance. Its high place in the American scale of values
may, indeed, be one determinant of our emotional retarda-
tion, our perpetual juvenility, and, more recently, of our
deficiency of first-order admirations, our incapacity for
high seriousness.

Henry A. Murray

Dieu a tout fait de rien. Mais le rien perce.

God made everything out of nothing. But the nothingness
shows through.

Paul Valéry

The nearer the Church, the further from God.

John Ray

In the beginning, we had the land and the white man had the
Bible. Then we had the Bible and the white man had the
land.

African saying

Had I been present at the Creation, I would have given some useful hints for the better ordering of the universe.

Alfonso the Learned

Most people really believe that the Christian commandments (e.g., love one's neighbor as oneself) are intentionally a little too severe—like putting the clock ahead half an hour to make sure of not being late in the morning.

Sören Kierkegaard

Henry Pritchett liked to tell a story about a man who was approached by a missionary for a contribution. The man protested that he was in debt, and the missionary said: "Don't you know that you owe more to God than to anyone else?" The man pondered this for a moment and then said, "Yes, but God isn't pressing me."

When I hear a man preach, I like to see him act as if he were fighting bees.

Abraham Lincoln

O Lord, how many read the Word, and yet from vice are not deterred!

Anonymous

No rage is equal to the rage of a contented right-thinking man when he is confronted in the market place by an idea which belongs in the pulpit.

Thurman W. Arnold

A man who should act, for one day, on the supposition that all the people about him were influenced by the religion which they professed would find himself ruined by night.

Thomas Macaulay

Defoe says that there were a hundred thousand stout country-fellows in his time ready to fight to the death against popery, without knowing whether popery was a man or a horse.

William Hazlitt

Father was always trying to bring this or that good thing to pass, only to find that there were obstacles in the way. . . . He didn't actually accuse God of gross inefficiency, but when he prayed his tone was loud and angry, like that of a dissatisfied guest in a carelessly managed hotel.

Clarence Day

I [have] often said that the best argument I knew for an immortal life was the existence of a man who deserved one.

William James

But too many people now climb onto the cross merely to be seen from a greater distance, even if they have to trample somewhat on the one who has been there so long.

Albert Camus

We have just enough religion to make us hate, but not enough to make us love one another.

Jonathan Swift

Of Joseph, the old man-servant: "He was, and is yet most likely, the wearisomest self-righteous Pharisee that ever ransacked the Bible to rake the promises to himself and fling the curses to his neighbours."

Emily Brontë

Saints need sinners.

Alan Watts

A genuine first-hand religious experience . . . is bound to be a heterodoxy to its witnesses, the prophet appearing as a mere lonely madman. If his doctrine proves contagious enough to spread to any others, it becomes a definite and labeled heresy. But if it then still proves contagious enough to triumph over persecution, it becomes itself an orthodoxy; and when a religion has become an orthodoxy, its day of inwardness is over: the spring is dry; the faithful live at second hand exclusively and stone the prophets in their turn. The new church . . . can be henceforth counted on as a staunch ally in every attempt to stifle the spontaneous religious spirit, and to stop all later bubblings of the fountain from which in purer days it drew its own supply of inspiration. . . . The baseness so commonly charged to religion's account [is] thus . . . not chargeable at all to religion proper, but rather to religion's wicked practical partner, the spirit of corporate dominion. And the bigotries are most of them . . . chargeable to religion's wicked intellectual partner, the spirit of dogmatic dominion, the passion for laying down the law in the form of an absolutely closed-in theoretic system.

William James

We are overrun with Popes. From curates and governesses, who may claim a sort of professional standing, to parents and uncles and nursery-maids and school teachers and wise-acres generally, there are scores of thousands of human insects groping through our darkness by the feeble phosphorescence of their own tails, yet ready at a moment's notice to reveal the will of God on every possible subject; to explain how and why the universe was made (in my youth they added the exact date) and the circumstances under which it will cease to exist; to lay down precise rules of right and wrong conduct; to discriminate infallibly between virtuous and vicious character; and all this with such certainty that they are prepared to visit all the rigors of the law, and all the ruinous penalties of social ostracism on people, however harmless their actions may be who venture to laugh

at their monstrous conceit or to pay their assumptions the
extravagant compliment of criticizing them.

George Bernard Shaw

A Unitarian is a person who believes there is, at most, one
God.

Alfred North Whitehead

An atheist may be simply one whose faith and love are con-
centrated on the impersonal aspects of God.

Simone Weil

Huxley coined the word "agnostic," he tells us, because
tolerably early in life he discovered that one of the un-
pardonable sins was for a man to presume to go about
unlabelled. "The world regards such a person as the police
do an unmuzzled dog, not under proper control. I could
find no label to suit me, so, in my desire to range myself and
be respectable, I invented one; and, as the chief thing I was
sure of was that I did not know a great many things that
the ——ists and the ——ites about me professed to be
familiar with, I called myself an Agnostic."

Cyril Bibby

I was much cheered on my arrival [in prison] by the warden at the gate, who had to take particulars about me. He asked my religion, and I replied "agnostic." He asked how to spell it, and remarked with a sigh, "Well, there are many religions, but I suppose they all worship the same God."

Bertrand Russell

The power of God man's arrogance shall not limit:
Sleep who takes all in his net takes not this,
Nor the unflagging months of Heaven—ageless the Master
Holds forever the shimmering courts of Olympus
    For time approaching, and time hereafter,
    And time forgotten, one rule stands:
    That greatness never
Shall touch the life of man without destruction.

Sophocles

Let him who believes in immortality enjoy his happiness in silence, without giving himself airs about it.

J. W. Goethe

He did not think, with the Caliph Omar Ben Adalaziz, that it was necessary to make a hell of this world to enjoy paradise in the next.

William Beckford

The opposite of the religious fanatic is not the fanatical atheist but the gentle cynic who cares not whether there is a God or not.

Eric Hoffer

. . . the refusal to choose is a form of choice, disbelief is a form of belief.

Frank Barron

It was said of one zealous apostle of free thought . . . that he would believe anything, so long as it was not in the Bible.

Gordon Allport

There's nothing more irritating than a Savior when you aren't ready to be saved.

D. Sutten

If you don't believe in the gods, leave them alone.

Chinese proverb

Dios tarda pero no olvida.
God delays but doesn't forget.

Spanish proverb

That which God writes on thy forehead, thou wilt come
to it.

The Koran

If God lived on earth, people would break his windows.

Yiddish proverb

Truth rests with God alone, and a little bit with me.

Yiddish proverb

The danger past and God forgotten.

John Ray

May the road rise with you
And the wind be ever at your back
And may the Lord hold you in the hollow of His hand.

Gaelic blessing

NINE

Good and Evil

"Marks of Weakness, Marks of Woe"

I wander thro' each charter'd street,
Near where the charter'd Thames does flow,
And mark in every face I meet
Marks of weakness, marks of woe.

In every cry of every Man,
In every Infant's cry of fear,
In every voice, in every ban,
The mind-forg'd manacles I hear. . . .

William Blake

Life in itself is neither a good nor an evil; it is the scene of good and evil.

Seneca

There are bad people who would be less dangerous if they were quite devoid of goodness.

La Rochefoucauld

The malevolent have secret teeth.

Publius Syrus

The Sun is never the worse for shining on a Dunghill.

Thomas Fuller

The greater part of what my neighbors call good I believe
in my soul to be bad, and if I repent of anything, it is very
likely to be my good behavior. What daemon possessed me
that I behaved so well?

Henry David Thoreau

. . . all men make mistakes
But a good man yields when he knows his course is wrong,
And repairs the evil. The only crime is pride.

Sophocles

Belinda: Ay, but you know we must return good for evil.
Lady Brute: That may be a mistake in the translation.

John Vanbrugh

When a good man is hurt all who would be called good
must suffer with him.

Euripides

If you are standing upright, don't worry if your shadow is
crooked.

Chinese Proverb

Hell will never have its due till it have you.

Thomas Fuller

Nothing is more unpleasant than a virtuous person with a mean mind.

Walter Bagehot

It's a hard, sad life for most people. Don't scorn the simple things that give them pleasure.

D. Sutten

The most melancholy of human reflections, perhaps, is that, on the whole, it is a question whether the benevolence of mankind does more harm than good.

Walter Bagehot

If rascals knew the advantages of virtue they would become honest men out of rascality.

Benjamin Franklin

We all are ready to be savage in some cause. The difference between a good man and bad one is the choice of the cause.

William James

Honesty is the best policy; but he who is governed by that maxim is not an honest man.

Richard Whately

A liar isn't believed even when he speaks the Truth.

German proverb

Hypocrisy is a Sort of Homage, that Vice pays to Virtue.

La Rochefoucauld

A little truth helps the lie go down.

Italian proverb

I am for integrity, if only because life is very short and truth is hard to come by.

Kermit Eby

Real strength never impairs beauty or harmony, but it often bestows it; and in everything imposingly beautiful, strength has much to do with the magic. . . .

Herman Melville

The first thing to learn in intercourse with others is non-interference with their own peculiar ways of being happy, provided those ways do not assume to interfere by violence with ours. No one has insight into all the ideals. No one should presume to judge them offhand. The pretension to dogmatize about them in each other is the root of most human injustices and cruelties, and the trait in human character most likely to make the angels weep.

William James

The common idea that success spoils people by making them vain, egotistic, and self-complacent is erroneous; on the contrary, it makes them, for the most part, humble, tolerant, and kind. Failure makes people cruel and bitter.

Somerset Maugham

The heroic hours of life do not announce their presence by drum and trumpet, challenging us to be true to ourselves by appeals to the martial spirit that keeps the blood at heat. Some little, unassuming, unobtrusive choice presents itself before us slyly and craftily, glib and insinuating, in the modest garb of innocence. To yield to its blandishments is so easy. The wrong, it seems, is venial. . . . Then it is that you will be summoned to show the courage of adventurous youth.

Benjamin Cardozo

Virtue will have nought to do with ease. . . . It demands a rough and thorny path.

Montaigne

To be good is noble; but to show others how to be good is nobler and no trouble.

Mark Twain

To ground the reward of virtuous actions on others' approval is to choose a too uncertain and shaky foundation. Especially in an age so corrupt and ignorant as this. . . . Whom can you trust to see what is praiseworthy? God defend me from being an honest man according to the ideas of honesty which men every day ascribe to themselves!

Montaigne

I have learned that I cannot dispose of other people's facts; but I possess such a key to my own as persuades me, against all their denials, that they also have a key to theirs. A sympathetic person is placed in the dilemma of a swimmer among drowning men, who all catch at him, and if he give so much as a leg or a finger they will drown him. They wish to be saved from the mischiefs of their vices, but not from their vices.

Ralph Waldo Emerson

When no wind blows, even the weathervane has character.

Stanislaw J. Lec

The Puritans objected to bearbaiting not because it gave pain to the bear but because it gave pleasure to the spectators.

Thomas Macaulay

If I knew for a certainty that a man was coming to my house with the conscious design of doing me good, I should run for my life.

Henry David Thoreau

If it seems to me that he has not attained to virtue, and yet asserts that he has, I will reproach him for holding cheapest what is worth most, and dearer what is worth less. This I will do for old and young,—for every man I meet. . . .

Plato
(*Socrates in* The Apology)

The wicked flee when no man pursueth—but they make better time when the righteous are after them.

Charles Henry Parkhurst

Video meliora proboque; deteriora sequor.
I see the better course and approve it; I follow the worse.

Ovid

Many without punishment, none without sin.

John Ray

. . . malice will always find bad motives for good actions.
Shall we therefore never do good?

Thomas Jefferson

Always do right. This will gratify some people and astonish
the rest.

Mark Twain

Conscience is the inner voice that warns us somebody may
be looking.

H. L. Mencken

All I maintain is that on this earth there are pestilences and
there are victims, and it's up to us, as far as possible, not to
join forces with the pestilences.

Albert Camus

Forsaking beauty and the sensual happiness attached to it, exclusively serving misfortune, calls for a nobility I lack. But, after all, nothing is true that forces one to exclude. Isolated beauty ends up simpering; solitary justice ends up oppressing. Whoever aims to serve one exclusive of the other serves no one, not even himself, and eventually serves injustice twice.

Albert Camus

There are men whom a happy disposition, a strong desire of glory and esteem, inspire with the same love for justice and virtue which men in general have for riches and honors. . . . But the number of these men is so small that I only mention them in honor of humanity.

Helvetius

If mankind had wished for what is right, they might have had it long ago.

William Hazlitt

Evil is a hill, every one gets on his own and speaks about someone else's.

African proverb

Evil knows the sleeping place of evil.

African proverb

Many foxes grow gray, but few grow good.

Benjamin Franklin

Omnis enim qui male agit odit lucem.

Everyone that doeth evil hateth the light.

John 3:20

Well, this is what we must overcome first of all. Our poisoned hearts must be cured. And the most difficult battle to be won against the enemy in the future must be fought within ourselves, with an exceptional effort that will transform our appetite for hatred into a desire for justice.

Albert Camus

Wolsey:
Cromwell, I charge thee, fling away ambition:
By that sin fell the angels; how can man, then,
The image of his Maker, hope to win by it?
Love thyself last: cherish those hearts that hate thee;
Corruption wins not more than honesty.
Still in thy right hand carry gentle peace,
To silence envious tongues. Be just, fear not. . . .

William Shakespeare

The "sentimentalist fallacy" is to shed tears over abstract justice and generosity, beauty, etc., and never to know these qualities when you meet them in the street, because the circumstances make them vulgar.

William James

For we knew only too well:
Even the hatred of squalor
Makes the brow grow stern.
Even anger against injustice
Makes the voice grow harsh. Alas, we
Who wished to lay the foundations of kindness
Could not ourselves be kind.

Bertolt Brecht

Whoever battles with monsters had better see that it does not turn him into a monster. And if you gaze long into an abyss, the abyss will gaze back into you.

Friedrich Nietzsche

If afflictions refine some, they consume others.

John Ray

Virtue does not always demand a heavy sacrifice—only the willingness to make it when necessary.

Frederick Dunn

All that is necessary for the forces of evil to win in the world is for enough good men to do nothing.

Edmund Burke

Where there is no shame, there is no honor.

African proverb

Al bien, buscarlo
y al mal, esperarlo.

For the good, search;
For the bad, await.

Spanish proverb

TEN

The Inner Life

"Where All Is Allowed, Where All Is Concealed"

Any man may play his part in the mummery, and act the honest man on the scaffolding; but to be right within, in his own bosom, where all is allowed, where all is concealed —there's the point! The next step is to be so in our own home, in our ordinary actions, of which we need render no account to any man, where there is no study, no make-believe.

Montaigne

It is not only for an exterior show or ostentation that our soul must play her part, but inwardly within ourselves, where no eyes shine but ours.

Montaigne

Caras vemos, corazones no sabemos.

Faces we see, hearts we know not.

Spanish proverb

There is no need to run outside
For better seeing, . . .
            . . . Rather abide
At the center of your being;
For the more you leave it, the less you learn.
Search your heart and see
. . .
The way to do is to be.

Lao-tzu

It is not only the most difficult thing to know oneself, but the most inconvenient one, too.

H. W. Shaw

Notre résurrection n'est pas tout entière dans le futur, elle est aussi en nous, elle commence, elle a déjà commencé.

Our resurrection does not lie wholly in the future; it is also within us, it is starting now, it has already started.

Paul Claudel

I care not so much what I am to others as I respect what I am in myself. I will be rich by myself and not by borrowing.

Montaigne

He whom God loves, hears, but he whom God hates, hears not. It is the heart that makes the owner into one that hears or one who hears not. His heart is a man's fortune. . . . As for a fool that hears not, he can do nothing at all. He regards knowledge as ignorance and good as bad. He lives on that of which one dies; his food is untruth.

Ptahhotep (ca. 2500 B.C.)

The more faithfully you listen to the voice within you, the better you will hear what is sounding outside. And only he who listens can speak.

Dag Hammarskjöld

Let not mercy and truth forsake thee: bind them about thy neck; write them upon the table of thine heart.

The Proverbs 3:3

Trust your heart. . . . Never deny it a hearing. It is the kind of house oracle that often foretells the most important.

Balthasar Gracian

By all means use sometimes to be alone.
Salute thy self: see what thy soul doth wear.
Dare to look in thy chest, for 'tis thine own:
And tumble up and down what thou find'st there.
     Who cannot rest till hee good-fellows finde,
     He breaks up house, turns out of doores his minde.

George Herbert

Many a time I have wanted to stop talking and find out what I really believed.

Walter Lippmann

By this, the dreamer crosses to the other shore. And by a like miracle, so will each whose work is the difficult, dangerous task of self-discovery and self-development be portered across the ocean of life.

     The multitude of men and women choose the less adventurous way of the comparatively unconscious civic and tribal routines. But these seekers, too, are saved—by virtue of the inherited symbolic aids of society, the rites of passage, the grace-yielding sacraments, given to mankind of old by the redeemers and handed down through millenniums. It is only those who know neither an inner call nor an outer doctrine whose plight truly is desperate; that is to say, most of us today, in this labyrinth without and within the heart.

Joseph Campbell

A real individual is self-substantial, a man who builds on his own genes for better or for worse, a man who would hate to be anybody but himself, a man who likes the flesh that sticks to his own ribs, a man who shows his natural face and does not care too much how others like it. A real individual consults himself, waits for the inner lift or fall of feeling, the dependable intimation, the touch of ages, the daemon's voice, the vital omen—and consults others only at the end of his own wits. He is apt to find that an idea ceases to be interesting as soon as it is generally accepted. He is a man who expands with joy in the heart of an enchanted isolation. He is a hive of surprising thoughts and judgments; it is not easy to predict what he will say.

Henry A. Murray

"Do this, do not do this; otherwise I will throw you into prison." Say that, and yours ceases to be a government over rational beings. Nay, rather, say, "As Zeus has ordained, do this; if you do not do so, you will be punished, you will suffer injury." What kind of injury? No injury but that

of not doing what you ought; you will destroy the man of
fidelity in you, the man of honor, the man of decent behavior. You need not look for greater injuries than these.

Epictetus

In proportion as our inward life fails, we go more con-
stantly and desperately to the post-office. You may depend
on it, that poor fellow who walks away with the greatest
number of letters, proud of his extensive correspondence,
has not heard from himself this long while.

Henry David Thoreau

. . . many of us who walk to and fro upon our usual tasks
are prisoners drawing mental maps of escape.

Loren Eiseley

You cannot endure yourselves and do not love yourselves
sufficiently; so you seek to entice your neighbor to love
you and gild yourselves with his error.

Friedrich Nietzsche

When a man is contented with himself and his own re-
sources, all is well. When he undertakes to play a part on
the stage, and to persuade the world to think more about
him than they do about themselves, he is got into a track

where he will find nothing but briars and thorns, vexation and disappointment.

William Hazlitt

Everyone constructs his own bed of nails.

D. Sutten

Of all the infirmities we have, the most savage is to despise our being.

Montaigne

What a man thinks of himself, that it is which determines, or rather indicates, his fate.

Henry David Thoreau

At every age and in every condition of life—even among those who enjoy affluence or occupy high posts, one encounters defeated people. Though they face the world with an air of assurance, they no longer believe that they can prevail or survive their own bad luck. The cause of their defeat may be brute circumstance or their own cynicism, or flagging energies, or self-indulgence, or fear or hatred or self-deception. Whatever the cause, they've given up.

D. Sutten

We are so accustomed to wearing a disguise before others that eventually we are unable to recognize ourselves.

La Rochefoucauld

I say, beware of all enterprises that require new clothes, and not rather a new wearer of clothes. If there is not a new man, how can the new clothes be made to fit? If you have any enterprise before you, try it in your old clothes.

Henry David Thoreau

Le coeur a ses raisons que la raison ne connaît point.

The heart has its reasons which reason knows nothing of.

Blaise Pascal

Hope is generally a wrong Guide, though it is very good company by the way.

Halifax

Hope is a good breakfast, but it is a bad supper.

Francis Bacon

Never anything here for my own secret delight; nothing for the hunger of the heart.

J. B. Priestley

Every man has a rainy corner in his life, from which bad
weather besets him.

Jean Paul Richter

Sorrow is like a precious treasure, shown only to friends.

African proverb

Every heart hath its own ache.

Thomas Fuller

It is my retreat and resting-place from the wars. I try to
keep this corner as a haven against the tempest outside, as I
do another corner in my soul.

Montaigne (of his home)

None knowes the weight of another's burthen.

George Herbert

Simple pleasures . . . are the last refuge of the complex.

Oscar Wilde

There is something in every person's character that cannot be broken—the bony structure of his character. Wanting to change it is the same as teaching a sheep to retrieve.

George C. Lichtenberg

Honor begets honor; trust begets trust; faith begets faith; and hope is the mainspring of life.

Henry L. Stimson

Character is much easier kept than recovered.

Thomas Paine

There is a form of eminence which does not depend on fate; it is an air which sets us apart and seems to portend great things; it is the value which we unconsciously attach to ourselves; it is the quality which wins us the deference of others; more than birth, position or ability, it gives us ascendency.

La Rochefoucauld

Beware of no Man more than thy self.

Thomas Fuller

The highest of characters, in my estimation, is his, who is as ready to pardon the moral errors of mankind, as if he were every day guilty of some himself; and at the same time as cautious of committing a fault as if he never forgave one.

Pliny the Younger

Pardon all but thy selfe.

George Herbert

One cannot too soon forget his errors and misdemeanors; for to dwell long upon them is to add to the offense, and repentance and sorrow can only be displaced by somewhat better, and which is as free and original as if they had not been.

Henry David Thoreau

Notice the difference between what happens when a man says to himself, "I have failed three times," and what happens when he says, "I am a failure."

S. I. Hayakawa

There comes a time when the thistles spring up over man's ruins with a sense of relief. It is as though the wasting away of power through time had brought with it the retreat of something shadowy and not untouched with evil. The tiny incremental thoughts of men tend to congeal in strange vast fabrics, from gladiatorial coliseums to skyscrapers, and then mutely demand release. In the end the mind rejects the hewn stone and rusting iron it has used as the visible expression of its inner dream. Instead it asks release for new casts at eternity, new opportunities to confine in fanes the uncapturable and elusive gods.

Loren Eiseley

Divine imaginings, like gods, come down to the groves of our Thessalies, and there, in the embrace of wild, dryad reminiscences, beget the beings that astonish the world.

Herman Melville

Everybody needs his memories. They keep the wolf of insignificance from the door.

Saul Bellow

Own only what you can always carry with you: know languages, know countries, know people. Let your memory be your travel bag.

Alexander Solzhenitsyn

Four ducks on a pond,
A grass-bank beyond,
A blue sky of spring,
White clouds on the wing:
What a little thing
To remember for years—
To remember with tears!

William Allingham

ELEVEN

Person to Person

"Love Your Enemies. It Makes Them So Damned Mad"

Love your enemies. It makes them so damned mad.

P. D. East

I was taught when I was young that if people would only love one another, all would be well with the world. This seemed simple and very nice; but I found when I tried to put it in practice not only that other people were seldom lovable, but that I was not very lovable myself.

George Bernard Shaw

Love and a cough cannot be hid.

George Herbert

To feed men and not to love them is to treat them as if they were barnyard cattle. To love them and not to respect them is to treat them as if they were household pets.

Mencius

Love consists in this, that two solitudes protect and touch and greet each other.

Rainer Maria Rilke

Love must be learned, and learned again and again; there is no end to it. Hate needs no instruction, but waits only to be provoked.

Katherine Ann Porter

The truth [is] that there is only one terminal dignity—love. And the story of a love is not important—what is important is that one is capable of love.

Helen Hayes

If you have one true Friend, you have more than your Share comes to.

Thomas Fuller

Friendship is almost always the union of a part of one mind with a part of another; people are friends in spots.

George Santayana

Life without a friend; death without a witness.

George Herbert

One should keep old roads and old friends.

German proverb

The best mirror is an old friend.

English proverb

You may poke a man's fire after you've known him for seven years.

English proverb

She is such a good friend that she would throw all her acquaintances into the water for the pleasure of fishing them out.

Talleyrand (of Mme. de Staël)

Cassius:
A friend should bear a friend's infirmities,
But Brutus makes mine greater than they are.

William Shakespeare

Jedermanns Gesell ist niemands Freund.
Everyone's companion is no one's friend.

German proverb

And if your friend does evil to you, say to him, "I forgive you for what you did to me, but how can I forgive you for what you did—to yourself?"

Friedrich Nietzsche

He who injured you is either stronger or weaker.
If he is weaker, spare him; if he is stronger, spare yourself.

Seneca

We always like those who admire us but we do not always like those whom we admire.

La Rochefoucauld

You can't eat your friends and have them too.

Budd Schulberg

Be on your guard . . . against those who confess as their weaknesses all the cardinal virtues.

Chesterfield

Men of great wit may be compared to a great fire, you can't get near enough to it to get warm without getting burnt.

H. W. Shaw

A mouth that praises and a hand that kills.

Arab proverb

Man is the only animal that can remain on friendly terms
with the victims he intends to eat until he eats them.

Samuel Butler

Many kisse the hand they wish cut off.

George Herbert

A wise man gets more use from his enemies than a fool from
his friends.

Balthasar Gracian

Ni todas las cosas se han de apurar, ni todos los amigos pro-
bar, ni todos los enemigos descubrir y declarar.
Not all things have to be scrutinized, nor all friends tested,
nor all enemies exposed and denounced.

Spanish proverb

No viper so little, but hath its Venom.

Thomas Fuller

There is no medicine to cure hatred.

African proverb

It is a sin peculiar to man to hate his victim.

Tacitus
(commenting on the fact that the Emperor Domitian
not only treated Agricola unjustly but disliked him)

More anger stems from lack of sleep than from all of life's frustrations.

D. Sutten

This is certain, that a man that studieth revenge keeps his wounds green, which otherwise would heal and do well. . . .

Francis Bacon

The best armor is to keep out of range.

Italian proverb

If you scatter thorns, don't go barefoot.

Italian proverb

Envy is thin because it bites but never eats.

Spanish proverb

Envy is more implacable than hatred.

La Rochefoucauld

Few of us can stand prosperity. Another man's, I mean.

Mark Twain

Vengeance is a dish that should be eaten cold.

English proverb

Nobuddy ever fergits where he buried a hatchet.

Kin Hubbard

Never contend with a man who has nothing to lose.

Balthasar Gracian

Never from obstinacy take the wrong side because your opponent has anticipated you in taking the right side.

Balthasar Gracian

All natural talk is a festival of ostentation; and by the laws of the game each accepts and fans the vanity of the other.

Robert Louis Stevenson

Mischief all comes from much opening of the mouth.

Chinese proverb

Thy friend has a friend, and thy friend's friend has a friend; be discreet.

The Talmud

If you don't say anything, you won't be called on to repeat it.

Calvin Coolidge

Who speaks ill of others to you will speak ill of you to others.

German proverb

What really flatters a man is that you think him worth flattering.

George Bernard Shaw

Many would be cowards if they had courage enough.

Thomas Fuller

It is an ordinary fault; we endeavor more that men should speak of us than how and what they speak, and it sufficeth us that our name run in men's mouths in what manner so-ever.

Montaigne

Dime de lo que blasonas, y te dire de lo que careces.

Tell me what you brag about and I'll tell you what you lack.

Spanish proverb

We only acknowledge small faults in order to make it appear that we are free from great ones.

La Rochefoucauld

No syren did ever so charm the ear of the listener, as the listening ear has charmed the soul of the syren.

Henry Taylor

My idea of an agreeable person is a person who agrees with me.

Benjamin Disraeli

When you say that you agree with a thing in principle you mean that you have not the slightest intention of carrying it out in practice.

Otto Von Bismarck

None are more readily taken with flattery than the proud who wish to be first but are not.

Spinoza

Flattery is counterfeit money which, but for vanity, would have no circulation.

La Rochefoucauld

I hate careless flattery, the kind that exhausts you in your effort to believe it.

Wilson Mizner

I much prefer a compliment, even if insincere, to sincere criticism.

Plautus

A man's intelligence does not increase as he acquires power. What does increase is the difficulty of telling him so.

D. Sutten

The most useful Part of Wisdom is for a Man to give a good guess what others think of him.

It is a dangerous thing to guess partially, and a melancholy thing to guess right.

Halifax

'Tis by no means the least of life's rules: To let things alone.

Balthasar Gracian

A Man that should call every thing by its right Name, would hardly pass the Streets without being knocked down as a common Enemy.

Halifax

Tact consists in knowing how far to go in going too far.

Jean Cocteau

Tact is the intelligence of the heart.

Anonymous

Find the grain of truth in criticism—chew it and swallow it.

D. Sutten

Many promising reconciliations have broken down because, while both parties came prepared to forgive, neither party came prepared to be forgiven.

Charles Williams

Si me muero, le perdono; si me alivio, ya veremos.

If I die, I forgive you; if I recover, we shall see.

Spanish proverb

Almost everyone takes pleasure in repaying small obligations; many are grateful for moderate acts of kindness; but scarcely anyone is thankful for great mercies.

La Rochefoucauld

A too quick Return of an Obligation is a sort of Ingratitude.

Thomas Fuller

Shy and proud men . . . are more liable than any others to fall into the hands of parasites and creatures of low character. For in the intimacies which are formed by shy men, they do not choose, but are chosen.

Henry Taylor

Very few individuals deserve to be listened to, but all deserve that our curiosity with regard to them should be a pitiful curiosity—that the insight we bring to bear on them should be charged with humility.

Amiel

Among the smaller duties of life I hardly know any one more important than that of not praising where praise is not due.

Sydney Smith

Never trust a man who speaks well of everybody.

Churton Collins

Si quieres que otro se ría
cuenta tus penas, María.

If you want to make someone laugh,
tell him your troubles, Maria.

Spanish proverb

Patience is a most necessary qualification for business; many a man would rather you heard his story than granted his request.

Chesterfield

Keep away from people who try to belittle your ambitions. Small people always do that, but the really great make you feel that you, too, can become great.

Mark Twain

I know no harder practical question than how much self-ishness one ought to stand from a gifted person for the sake of his gifts or on the chance of his being right in the long run. The Superman will certainly come like a thief in the night, and be shot at accordingly; but we cannot leave our property wholly undefended on that account.

George Bernard Shaw

Self-sacrifice enables us to sacrifice other people without blushing.

George Bernard Shaw

A man whom no one pleases is much worse off than a man who pleases no one.

La Rochefoucauld

There is no more subtle maneuver than to pretend to fall into the snares that other people set for us; one is never so easily fooled as when one thinks one is fooling others.

La Rochefoucauld

If a person has no delicacy, he has you in his power.

William Hazlitt

I will have nought to do with a man who can blow hot and cold with the same breath.

Aesop

Nothing astonishes men so much as common sense and plain dealing.

Ralph Waldo Emerson

Quien da el pan impone la ley.
Who gives the bread lays down the law.

Spanish proverb

It is difficult to get a man to understand something when his salary depends upon his not understanding it.

Upton Sinclair

Even the blind can see money.

Chinese proverb

Only the rich have distant relatives.

Chinese proverb

One would be in less danger
From the wiles of the stranger
If one's own kin and kith
Were more fun to be with.

Ogden Nash

One half the world laughs at the other, and fools are they
all.

Balthasar Gracian

Some people can stay longer in an hour than others can
in a week.

William Dean Howells

The great pleasure of a dog is that you may make a fool
of yourself with him and not only will he not scold you,
but he will make a fool of himself too.

Samuel Butler

TWELVE

The Human Comedy

"Happiness Is No Laughing Matter"

Happiness is no laughing matter.

Richard Whately

The course of true anything never does run smooth.

Samuel Butler

If every man stuck to his talent the cows would be well tended.

J. P. DeFlorian

I doubt if the vigilance of the law is equal to making money stick by overcredulous people.

Justice Robert H. Jackson

A wager is a fool's argument.

Thomas Fuller

So there I sat and smoked my cigar. . . . "You are going on," I said to myself, "to become an old man, without being anything, and without really undertaking to do anything. On the other hand, wherever you look about you, in literature and in life, you see . . . the many benefactors of the age who know how to benefit mankind by making life

easier and easier. . . . And what are you doing?" . . . and
then suddenly this thought flashed through my mind: "You
must do something, but inasmuch as with your limited ca-
pacities it will be impossible to make anything easier . . .
you must with the same humanitarian enthusiasm . . . undertake to make something harder." . . . it flattered me to
think that I would be loved and esteemed by the whole
community. For when all combine in every way to make
everything easier, there remains only one possible danger,
namely, that the ease becomes so great that it becomes altogether too great; then there is only one want left, . . .
people will want difficulty. Out of love for mankind, and
out of despair at my embarrassing situation . . . I con-
ceived it as my task to create difficulties everywhere.

Sören Kierkegaard

Who hath no head, needes no hatt.

George Herbert

Newfoundland dogs are good to save children from drowning, but you must have a pond of water handy and a child,
or else there will be no profit in boarding a Newfoundland.

H. W. Shaw

Believe me, for certain men at least, not taking what one
doesn't desire is the hardest thing in the world.

Albert Camus

If you haven't all the things you want, be grateful for the things you don't have that you didn't want.

Anonymous

There is no pleasure in having nothing to do; the fun is in having lots to do and not doing it.

John W. Raper

The most trying fools are the bright ones.

La Rochefoucauld

Definition of a lawyer's function: To protect his clients from being persuaded by persons whom they do not know to enter into contracts which they do not understand to purchase goods which they do not want with money which they have not got.

Lord Greene

I feel myself bound to state that I must, when I decided that case, have seen it in a point of view, in which, after most laborious consideration, I cannot see it now.

Lord Eldon (in a legal decision)

I have seen hypocrisy that was so artful that it was good judgment to be deceived by it.

H. W. Shaw

There are people who exaggerate so much that they can't tell the truth without lying.

H. W. Shaw

If they really want to honor the boys, why don't they let them sit in the stands and have the people march by?

Will Rogers
(on World War I homecoming parades)

Oh, I wish I were a miser; being a miser is so occupying.

Gertrude Stein

As a cousin of mine once said about money, money is always there but the pockets change; it is not in the same pockets after a change, and that is all there is to say about money.

Gertrude Stein

If you cannot get rid of the family skeleton, you may as well make it dance.

George Bernard Shaw
(speaking of his family's habit of laughing over
his father's drunken escapades)

Once in every half-century, at longest, a family should be merged into the great, obscure mass of humanity, and forget all about its ancestors.

Nathaniel Hawthorne

Sometimes men come by the name of genius in the same way that certain insects come by the name of centipede—not because they have a hundred feet, but because most people can't count above fourteen.

George C. Lichtenberg

The ugliest of trades have their moments of enjoyment. If I were a gravedigger, or even a hangman, there are some people I could work for with a good deal of enjoyment.

Douglas Jerrold

I have finally come to the conclusion that if I can't prove a thing without betting $5 on it, the thing's got a dreadful weak spot somewhere.

H. W. Shaw

People have to talk about something just to keep their voice boxes in working order, so they'll have good voice boxes in case there's ever anything really meaningful to say.

Kurt Vonnegut, Jr.

I like work; it fascinates me. I can sit and look at it for hours. I love to keep it by me: the idea of getting rid of it nearly breaks my heart.

Jerome K. Jerome

So live that you wouldn't be ashamed to sell the family parrot to the town gossip.

Will Rogers

THIRTEEN

Writers and Writing

"Learn as Much by Writing as by Reading"

≈ ≈ ≈

Learn as much by writing as by reading.

Lord Acton

For good or ill, I am an ignorant man, almost a poet, and I can only spread a feast of what everybody knows.

George Santayana

I write verses myself, but I have no sympathy with the notion that the world owes a duty to poetry, or any other art. Poetry is not a civilizer, rather the reverse, for great poetry appeals to the most primitive instincts. It is not necessarily a moralizer; it does not necessarily improve one's character; it does not even teach good manners. It is a beautiful work of nature, like an eagle or a high sunrise. You owe it no duty. If you like it, listen to it; if not, let it alone.

Robinson Jeffers

As a general rule, run your pen through every other word you have written; you have no idea what vigor it will give to your style.

Sydney Smith

Only kings, editors, and people with tapeworm have the right to use the editorial "we."

Mark Twain

No author dislikes to be edited as much as he dislikes not to be published.

Russell Lynes

The writer who can't at times throw away a thought about which another would have written dissertations, unworried whether or not the reader will find it, will never become a great writer.

George C. Lichtenberg

I will . . . endeavor never to write more clearly than I think.

Niels Bohr

To place before mankind the common sense of the subject, [in] terms so plain and firm as to command their assent and to justify ourselves in the independent stand we [were] compelled to take.

Thomas Jefferson
(on his objectives in drafting the
Declaration of Independence)

The quarrel is a very pretty quarrel as it stands; we should only spoil it by trying to explain it.

R. Brinsley Sheridan

A well-written life is almost as rare as a well spent one.
Thomas Carlyle

His biography [*Lord Lyndhurst*] has been written by Lord
Campbell, and fully justified what Lyndhurst said when he
heard that it was contemplated, that the prospect added
another pang to death.
Serjeant Ballantine

It is the glory and merit of some men to write well and of
others not to write at all.
Jean de La Bruyère

Here we write well when we expose frauds and hypocrites.
We are great at counting warts and blemishes and weighing
feet of clay. In expressing love, we belong among the un-
developed countries.
Saul Bellow

. . . the young man or woman writing today has forgotten
the problems of the human heart in conflict with itself. He
must learn them again. He must teach himself that the
basest of all things is to be afraid; and, teaching himself that,
forget it forever, leaving no room in his workshop for anything but the old verities and truths of the heart. Until he

does so, he labors under a curse. He writes not of love but
of lust, of defeats in which nobody loses anything of value,
of victories without hope and, worst of all, without pity or
compassion. His griefs grieve on no universal bones, leaving
no scars. He writes not of the heart but of the glands.

   Until he relearns these things, he will write as though
he stood alone and watched the end of man. I decline to accept the end of man. It is easy enough to say that man is
immortal simply because he will endure; that when the last
ding-dong of doom has clanged and faded from the last
worthless rock hanging tideless in the last red and dying
evening, that even then there will still be one more sound:
that of his puny inexhaustible voice, still talking. I refuse to
accept this. I believe that man will not merely endure; he
will prevail.

William Faulkner

On the literary scene today criticism is the main show. A
writer is an important writer if he supplies something that
living critics need for the fullness of their intellectual life
and the documenting of their pet views.

D. Sutten

I couldn't write the things they publish now, with no beginning and no end, and a little incest in the middle.

Irvin S. Cobb

A deluge of words and a drop of sense.

John Ray

I sometimes doubt that a writer should refine or improve his workroom by so much as a dictionary: one thing leads to another and the first thing you know he has a stuffed chair and is fast asleep in it.

E. B. White

A man must not write on Plato unless he has spent so much of his youth on Greek as to have had no time for the things that Plato thought important.

Bertrand Russell

In every work of genius we recognize our own rejected thoughts; they come back to us with a certain alienated majesty.

Ralph Waldo Emerson

To give an accurate and exhaustive account of that period would need a far less brilliant pen than mine.

Max Beerbohm

Gertrude was never polite to anything but material: when she patted someone on the head you could be sure that the head was about to appear, smoked, in her next novel.

Randall Jarrell

Every journalist has a novel in him, which is an excellent place for it.

Russell Lynes

My friend: when a man has anything to tell in this world, the difficulty is not to make him tell it, but to prevent him from telling it too often.

George Bernard Shaw

Hawthorne was out of touch with his time, and he will be out of touch with any time. He thought man was immortal: a mistake made only by the greatest writers.

Mark Van Doren

A book is a mirror: when a monkey looks in, no apostle can look out.

George C. Lichtenberg

Many brave men lived before Agamemnon, but all unwept and unknown they sleep in endless night, for they had no poets to sound their praises.

Horace

This is a work too hard for the teeth of time, and cannot perish but in the general flames, when all things shall confess their ashes.

Thomas Browne

It is said . . . that Liszt got Verdi to give him a letter of introduction to Rossini and went to call on him. Rossini was exceedingly polite, asked him to play, and when he had done inquired what the piece was. Liszt said, "It is a march I have written on the death of Meyerbeer, how do you like it, maestro?" Rossini said he liked it very much, but presently added, "Do you not think it would have been better if it had been you who had died, and Meyerbeer who had written the music?"

Samuel Butler

FOURTEEN

In a Manner of Speaking

"Ah, Mr. Smith, Ye've Such a Way of Putting Things"

Dr. Doyle argued against [Sydney] Smith's proposal that the Government should pay the Irish Catholic priests, saying that they would refuse it. Said Smith: "Do you mean to say that if every priest in Ireland received in tomorrow's mail a government letter with 100 pounds, 1st quarter of their year's income, that they would refuse it?"

"Ah, Mr. Smith," said Dr. Doyle, "ye've such a way of putting things."

An old story—one of those which are true and not true everywhere and nowhere—describes it as follows: The citizens of a certain town (Siena seems to be meant) had once an officer in their service who had freed them from foreign aggression; daily they took counsel how to recompense him and concluded that no reward in their power was great enough, not even if they made him lord of the city. At last one of them rose and said, "Let us kill him and then worship him as our patron saint." And so they did. . . .

Jacob Burckhardt

There are not ten men in Boston equal to Shakespeare.

An unidentified Bostonian quoted by W. E. Gladstone

The old lady's comment on the Great Depression: "What a pity this old depression had to come along just when times are so bad."

Carl Becker

It is discouraging to try to penetrate a mind like yours.
You ought to get it out and dance on it. That would take
some of the rigidity out of it. . . . You really must get
your mind out and have it repaired; you see, yourself, that
it is all caked together.

Mark Twain
(in a letter to a man who had the presumption to edit
his introduction to the Joan of Arc Trials)

An event has happened, upon which it is difficult to speak,
and impossible to be silent.

Edmund Burke
(on the impeachment of Warren Hastings in 1789)

I will look, your Honor, and endeavor to find a precedent,
if you require it; though it would seem to be a pity that the
Court should lose the honor of being the first to establish
so just a rule.

Rufus Choate

Tears have always been considered legitimate arguments
before a jury, and while the question has never arisen out
of any such behavior in this Court, we know of no rule or
jurisdiction in the Court below to check them. It would
appear to be one of the natural rights of counsel, which no
Court or constitution could take away. It is certainly, if
no more, a matter of the highest personal privilege. Indeed,

if counsel has them at command, it may be seriously questioned whether it is not his professional duty to shed them whenever proper occasion arises, and the trial Judge would not feel constrained to interfere unless they were indulged in to such excess as to impede or delay the business of the Court.

Justice John S. Wilkes

Coke: Mr. Bacon, if you have any tooth against me, pluck it out, for it will do you more hurt than all the teeth in your head will do you good.
Bacon: Mr. Attorney, I respect you: I fear you not: and the less you speak of your own greatness, the more I will think of it.

Francis Bacon
(recounted in a letter to Cecil)

The distance is nothing; it is only the first step that is difficult.

Marquise du Deffand
(commenting on the story that St. Denis, carrying his head in his hands, walked two leagues)

When Wilson was carrying out his reforms at Princeton, . . . he demanded enormous power from the trustees. One of these said to him one day, "Mr. President, don't you think it would be better to persuade these men gradually . . . rather than to demand such coercive measures?"

"Why," Wilson is quoted saying in reply, "how can I democratize this college unless I have absolute authority?"

Henry S. Pritchett

I am reminded of the episode of Reed Smoot, the first Senator to be elected from Utah. He was a Mormon, and several Senators protested to Boies Penrose, then the leader of the Senate, that he should not be allowed to take his seat. Penrose asked whether Smoot had more than one wife and, on being told that he had only one, looked out over the Senate and said: "Well, I don't see why we can't get along just as well with a polygamist who doesn't polyg as we do with a lot of monogamists who don't monog!"

Francis T. P. Plimpton

"You oughtn't to yield to temptation."
"Well, somebody must, or the thing becomes absurd."

Anthony Hope

Se non è vero, è molto ben trovato.
If it isn't true, it is a happy invention.

Italian proverb

Sheridan's parliamentary colleagues had brought in an extremely unpopular measure, on which they were defeated.

He then said, that he had often heard of people knocking out their brains against a wall; but never before known of anyone building a wall expressly for the purpose.

Walter Jerrold
(of R. Brinsley Sheridan)

Sheridan, the first time he met his son Tom after the latter's marriage, was seriously angry with him, and told him that he had made his will and cut him off with a shilling.

Tom said that he was indeed very sorry, and immediately added, "You don't happen to have the shilling about you now, sir, do you?"

Walter Jerrold
(of R. Brinsley Sheridan)

The government was contemplating the dispatch of an expedition to Burma, with a view to taking Rangoon, and a question arose as to who would be the fittest general to be sent in command of the expedition. The Cabinet sent for the Duke of Wellington, and asked his advice. He instantly replied, "Send Lord Combermere."

"But we have always understood that your Grace thought Lord Combermere a fool."

"So he is a fool, and a damned fool; but he can take Rangoon."

G. W. E. Russell

The following incidents will give one an idea of [Wayland's] manner in the classroom. One day a rather conceited man said in the class when Dr. Wayland was speaking of the great wisdom of the Proverbs in the Scriptures, "I do not think there is anything very remarkable in the Proverbs. They are rather commonplace remarks of common people." "Very well," replied the Doctor, "Make one."

James Burrill Angell
(of Francis Wayland)

Sir George Beaumont was standing before a famous painting beside [Sydney] Smith. Sir George, gazing at the painting, exclaimed, "Immense breadth of light and shade!" Smith said innocently, "Yes, about an inch and a half."

Walter Jerrold

I don't know what effect these men will have upon the enemy, but, by God, they terrify me.

Arthur Wellesley, Duke of Wellington
(on a draft of troops sent to him in Spain, 1809)

I can govern the United States or I can govern my daughter Alice, but I can't do both.

Theodore Roosevelt

Any manager who can't get along with a .400 hitter is
crazy.

Joe McCarthy
(of the New York Yankees)

I would rather have men ask, after I am dead, why I have
no monument than why I have one.

Cato the Elder

Catching a fly ball is a pleasure but knowing what to do
with it is a business.

Tommy Henrich
(of the New York Yankees)

If I owned Hell and Texas I'd rent out Texas and live in
Hell.

P. H. Sheridan

Early in his administration, [President Arthur Twining
Hadley of Yale] and President Eliot were attending the
inauguration of another college president. Eliot said to the

new incumbent: "Now that you are president you are fair game for all newspapers. They will take something you say today, dug up something to the contrary you said in the past, and claim that you are a liar." Hadley asked: "Why President Eliot, have they claimed that with you?" "Claimed it?" said Eliot, "They've proved it!"

Morris Hadley

Not all the Capitol chaplains were perfunctory. The Rev. Byron Sunderland, one day in April, 1864, invoked:

"O Lord, give us that Thou wilt in Thine infinite wisdom vouchsafe to our rulers and legislators in this Congress assembled more brains—more brains, Lord."

Noah Brooks

FIFTEEN

History

"The Day of Judgment Is Either Approaching or It Is Not"

The time was the 19th of May 1780. The place was Hartford, Connecticut. The day has gone down in New England history as a terrible foretaste of Judgment Day. For at noon the skies turned from blue to grey and by mid-afternoon had blackened over so densely that, in that religious age, men fell on their knees and begged a final blessing before the end came. The Connecticut House of Representatives was in session. And as some of the men fell down and others clamored for an immediate adjournment, the Speaker of the House, one Col. Davenport, came to his feet. He silenced them and said these words: "The day of judgment is either approaching or it is not. If it is not, there is no cause for adjournment. If it is, I choose to be found doing my duty. I wish therefore that candles may be brought."

Alistair Cooke

Historic continuity with the past is not a duty, it is only a necessity.

Oliver Wendell Holmes, Jr.

(One of the leaders of the Britons facing Agricola's army addressing his men): "We, the last men on earth, the last of the free, have been shielded till today by the very remoteness and the seclusion for which we are famed. . . . But today the boundary of Britain is exposed; beyond us lies no nation, nothing but waves and rocks and the Romans. . . . Brigands of the world . . . they create a desolation and call it peace.

Tacitus

Thursday, October 11

The course was west-southwest, and there was more sea than there had been during the whole of the voyage. They saw sandpipers, and a green reed near the ship. Those of the caravel *Pinta* saw a cane and a pole, and they took up another small pole which appeared to have been worked with iron; also another bit of cane, a land plant, and a small board. The crew of the caravel *Nina* also saw signs of land, and a small branch covered with berries. Everyone breathed afresh and rejoiced at these signs. After sunset the Admiral returned to his original west course. . . .

Up to two hours after midnight they had gone ninety miles (since sunset) equal to twenty-two and a half leagues. As the caravel *Pinta* was a better sailer and went ahead of the Admiral (who was aboard the *Santa Maria*), she found the land (2 a.m., Friday, October 12) and made the signals ordered by the Admiral.

Journal of Christopher Columbus

Upon the ninth of November (1620)

After many difficulties in boisterous storms, at length by God's providence, by break of the day we espied land which we deemed to be Cape Cod, and so afterward it proved. And the appearance of it much comforted us, especially, seeing so goodly a land, and wooded to the brink of the sea, it caused us to rejoice together and praise God.

Wm. Bradford and Edward Winslow

In short my dear Friend you and I have been indefatigable Labourers through our whole Lives for a Cause which will be thrown away in the next generation, upon the Vanity and Foppery of Persons of whom we do not now know the Names perhaps. —The War that is now breaking out will render our Country, whether she is forced into it, or not, rich, great and powerful in comparison of what she now is, and Riches Grandeur and Power will have the same effect upon American as it has upon European minds.

John Adams
(in a letter to Thomas Jefferson, October 9, 1787)

I am well aware of the toil, and blood, and treasure, that it will cost us to maintain this declaration, and support and defend these States. Yet, through all the gloom, I can see the rays of ravishing light and glory. . . . The second day of July, 1776, will be the most memorable epoch in the history of America. I am apt to believe that it will be celebrated by succeeding generations as the great anniversary festival. It ought to be commemorated as the day of deliverance, by solemn acts of devotion to God Almighty. It ought to be solemnized with pomp and parade, with shows, games, sports, guns, bells, bonfires, and illuminations, from one end of this continent to the other, from this time forward for evermore.

John Adams
(letter to Mrs. Adams, July 3, 1776)

Posterity! You will never know how much it cost the present generation to preserve your freedom! I hope you will make a good use of it. If you do not, I shall repent it in heaven that I ever took half the pains to preserve it.

John Adams
(letter to Mrs. Adams, April 26, 1777)

Unrestrained by law, or the fear of punishment, every deadly passion will have full scope, private quarrels will be revenged, and public feuds and rivalships will call forth the bitterest hate and vengeance. Neighbors will become enemies of neighbors, brothers of brothers, fathers of their sons, and sons of their fathers. Murder, robbery, rape, adultery, and incest will be openly taught and practised, the air will be rent with the cries of distress, the soil soaked with blood, and the nation black with crimes.

"Burleigh," Sept. 15, 1800
(predicting the consequences of electing Thomas Jefferson
to the Presidency)

We lost because we told ourselves we lost.

Leo Tolstoy
(War and Peace—Prince Andrey's comment on Austerlitz)

All was not lost until the moment when all had succeeded.

Napoleon Bonaparte
(on the anniversary of Waterloo)

The effect of liberty to individuals is that they may do what they please: we ought to see what it will please them to do, before we risk congratulations.

Edmund Burke
(*on the French Revolution*)

Old George Washington's forte was not to hev eny public man of the present day resemble him to eny alarmin extent.

Artemus Ward

I . . . had ambition not only to go farther than any man had ever been before, but as far as it was possible for a man to go.

Captain James Cook

In the early days of the Indian Territory, there were no such things as birth certificates. You being there was certificate enough.

Will Rogers

May 26, 1859
    To obtain a preemption, the squatter must swear that he actually resides on the quarter-section he applies for, has built a habitation and made other improvements there, and wants the land for his own use and that of his family.

The squatters who took possession of these lands must every one have committed gross perjury in obtaining pre-emption.

My friend informed me that every road I saw was "preempted," and held at thirty up to a hundred dollars or more per acre. "Preempted!" I exclaimed. "By living or lying?" "Well," he responded, "they live a little and lie a little."

Horace Greeley

June 21, 1859

The rival cities of Denver and Auraria front on each other from either bank of Cherry Creek, just before it is lost in the South Platte. Of these rival cities, Auraria is by far the most venerable—some of its structures being, I think, fully a year old, if not more.

Horace Greeley

In times like the present, men should utter nothing for which they would not willingly be responsible through time and eternity.

Abraham Lincoln

In 1872, Burckhardt writes to a friend: ". . . There is the prospect of long and voluntary submission to single leaders and usurpers. The people no longer believe in principles, but will probably periodically believe in saviours. Because

of this reason, authority will again raise its head in the delightful 20th century and a frightful head it will be."

Erich Fromm

Of all the days of the war, there are two especially I can
never forget. Those were the days following the news, in
New York and Brooklyn, of that first Bull Run defeat, and
the day of Abraham Lincoln's death. I was home in Brooklyn on both occasions. The day of the murder we heard the
news very early in the morning. Mother prepared breakfast
—and other meals afterward—as usual; but not a mouthful
was eaten all day by either of us. We each drank half a
cup of coffee; that was all. Little was said. We got every
newspaper morning and evening, and the frequent extras of
that period, and passed them silently to each other.

Walt Whitman

A great man represents a great ganglion in the nerves of
society, or, to vary the figure, a strategic point in the campaign of history, and part of his greatness consists in his
being *there.*

Oliver Wendell Holmes, Jr.
(on the 100th anniversary of the day John Marshall
took his seat as Chief Justice)

I apprehend for the next hundred years an ultimate, colos-
sal, cosmic collapse; but not on any of our old lines. My

belief is that science is to wreck us, and that we are like monkeys monkeying with a loaded shell; we don't in the least know or care where our practically infinite energies come from or will bring us to. . . . But the faintest disturbance of equilibrium is felt throughout the solar system, and I feel sure that our power over energy has now reached a point where it just sensibly effects the old adjustment. It is mathematically certain to me that another thirty years of energy-development at the rate of the last century, must reach an *impasse.*

Henry Adams (1902)

Success four flights Thursday morning all against twenty-one mile wind started from level with engine power alone average speed through air thirty-one miles longest 59 seconds inform press home Christmas.

Orville and Wilbur Wright
(telegram to their father, Kitty Hawk,
North Carolina, December 17, 1903)

When my brother and I built and flew the first man-carrying flying machine, we thought that we were introducing into the world an invention which would make further wars practically impossible. That we were not alone in this thought is evidenced by the fact that the French Peace Society presented us with medals on account of our invention. We thought governments would realize the impossibility of winning by surprise attacks, and that no country

would enter into war with another when it knew it would
have to win by simply wearing out the enemy.
Orville Wright, 1917

Beautiful city! so venerable, so lovely, so unravaged by the
fierce intellectual life of our century, so serene! . . .
whispering from her towers the last enchantments of the
Middle Ages. . . . Home of lost causes, and forsaken be-
liefs, and unpopular names, and impossible loyalties!
Matthew Arnold (of Oxford)

We won't really hear what was done at this conference
till we read one of the delegates' memoirs after the next
war.
Will Rogers
(on the 1930 Disarmament Conference)

Back at the right waist window, Sgt. Bob Shumard, the
assistant flight engineer, turned his polaroids to full intensity
and prepared to take advantage of the fact that he had the
best seat for the show. . . . He adjusted his polaroids to
mild intensity and looked down at Hiroshima. A large white
cloud was spreading rapidly over the whole area, obscuring
everything and rising very rapidly.
Robert Schwartz (August 1945)

When the Nazis invaded the Soviet Union, Winston Churchill was asked by his private secretary whether—as the leading British anti-Communist—he would find it embarrassing to be on the same side as the Soviets. Churchill said: "Not at all. I have only one purpose, the destruction of Hitler, and my life is much simplified thereby. If Hitler invaded Hell I would make at least a favorable reference to the Devil in the House of Commons."

The United States has never lost a war or won a conference.

Will Rogers

It is not everyone that finds the age he deserves. . . . Some men have been worthy of a better century. . . . Things have their period; even excellences are subject to fashion.

Balthasar Gracian

Every Age confutes old Errors, and begets new.

Thomas Fuller

The men of my profession speak frequently of the physical scars of evolution. They mean by this that we carry in our bodies evidence of the long way we have traveled. There is written even in our bones the many passages at arms upon the road. To the student of the past we are as scarred and ragged as old battle flags. We drag with us into the future the tatters of defeat as well as of victory: impulses of deep-buried animal aggressiveness, unconscious mid-brain rivalries that hurl us into senseless accidents upon the road, even as nations, which after all, are but a few men magnified, similarly destroy themselves upon the even more dangerous road of history.

Loren Eiseley

It's never safe to be nostalgic about something until you're absolutely certain there's no chance of its coming back.

Bill Vaughn

SIXTEEN

Change

"You Can't Step Twice into the Same River"

~ ~ ~

You cannot step twice into the same river, for other waters
are continually flowing on.

Heraclitus

Ogni giorno passa un giorno.

Each day a day goes by.

Carlo Goldoni

Civilization is a movement and not a condition, a voyage and
not a harbor.

Arnold Toynbee

It must be admitted that there is a degree of instability
which is inconsistent with civilization. But, on the whole,
the great ages have been unstable ages.

Alfred North Whitehead

It is the first step in sociological wisdom, to recognize that
the major advances in civilization are processes which all
but wreck the societies in which they occur. . . .

Alfred North Whitehead

No nation, no social institution, ever acquired coherence without some sort of a fight. Out of the fight come its myths and its heroes.

Thurman Arnold

The greatest invention of the nineteenth century was the invention of the method of invention. . . . In order to understand our epoch, we can neglect all the details of change, such as railways, telegraphs, radios, spinning machines, synthetic dyes. We must concentrate on the method itself; that is the real novelty, which has broken up the foundations of the old civilization.

Alfred North Whitehead

Men believe that a society is disintegrating when it can no longer be pictured in familiar terms. Unhappy is a people that has run out of words to describe what is going on.

Thurman Arnold

The traditionalist believes that foolishness frozen into custom is preferable to foolishness fresh off the vine.

D. Sutten

I have steadily endeavoured to keep my mind free so as to give up any hypothesis, however much beloved (and I cannot resist forming one on every subject), as soon as facts are shown to be opposed to it. Indeed, I have had no choice but to act in this manner, for with the exception of the Coral Reefs, I cannot remember a single first-formed hypothesis which had not after a time to be given up or greatly modified. This has naturally led me to distrust greatly deductive reasoning in the mixed sciences. On the other hand, I am not very sceptical—a frame of mind which I believe to be injurious to the progress of science. A good deal of scepticism in a scientific man is advisable to avoid much loss of time, but I have met with not a few men, who, I feel sure, have often thus been deterred from experiment or observations which would have proved directly or indirectly serviceable.

Charles Darwin

The reasonable man adapts himself to the world: the unreasonable one persists in trying to adapt the world to himself. Therefore all progress depends on the unreasonable man.

George Bernard Shaw

He that will not apply new remedies must expect new evils; for time is the greatest innovator; and if time of course alter things to the worse, and wisdom and counsel shall not alter them to the better what shall be the end?

Francis Bacon

Nothing is ever done until everyone is convinced that it ought to be done, and has been convinced for so long that it is now time to do something else.

F. M. Cornford

Senseless agencies (e.g. climatic changes, steam, the Barbarians) and formulated aspirations cooperate in the work of driving mankind from its old anchorage. Sometimes the period of change is an age of hope, sometimes it is an age of despair. When mankind has slipped its cables, sometimes it is bent on the discovery of a New World, and sometimes it is haunted by the dim sound of the breakers dashing on the rocks ahead.

Alfred North Whitehead

Each generation criticizes the unconscious assumptions made by its parents. It may assent to them, but it brings them out in the open.

Alfred North Whitehead

Those societies which cannot combine reverence to their symbols with freedom of revision, must ultimately decay either from anarchy, or from the slow atrophy of a life stifled by useless shadows.

Alfred North Whitehead

History warns us . . . that it is the customary fate of new truths to begin as heresies and to end as superstitions. . . .

T. H. Huxley

It is very easy to generate in a people a contempt for their ancient observances; no man ever attempted it without succeeding. But many have come to grief in their attempt to establish a better state of things in place of what they have destroyed.

Montaigne

There is no squabbling so violent as that between people who accepted an idea yesterday and those who will accept the same idea tomorrow.

Christopher Morley

If you cry "Forward" you must be sure to make clear the direction in which to go. Don't you see that if you fail to do that and simply call out the word to a monk and a revolutionary, they will go in precisely opposite directions.

Anton Chekhov

Plasticity loves new moulds because it can fill them, but for a man of sluggish mind and bad manners there is decidedly no place like home.

George Santayana

Only that which is provisional endures.

French proverb

Ils se sont seulement reculés pour mieux sauter.
They have only stepped back in order to leap farther.

Montaigne

Ouvrez les yeux! Le monde est encore intact.
Open your eyes! The world is still intact.

Paul Claudel

SEVENTEEN

Politics, Law, Government

"The Glad Hand and the Marble Heart"

∽ ∽ ∽

All the European countries are seeking to diminish the check upon individual spontaneity which state examinations with their tyrannous growth have brought in their train. We have had to institute state examinations too; and it will perhaps be fortunate if some day hereafter our descendants, comparing machine with machine, do not sigh with regret for old times and American freedom, and wish that the *regime* of the dear old bosses might be reinstalled, with plain human nature, the glad hand and the marble heart, liking and disliking, and man-to-man relations grown possible again.

William James

We are in bondage to the law in order that we may be free.

Cicero

Our system has the growth and development of human personality as its goal and we believe that choice is a way of learning and of growth and that it is better for men to choose for themselves even if they make the wrong decisions than it is to have those decisions made for them. We choose freedom, and freedom is not a solution of problems. It is a way of action that is in itself more important than the results.

Lyman Bryson

If there be any among us who would wish to dissolve this Union or to change its republican form, let them stand undisturbed as monuments of the safety with which error of opinion may be tolerated where reason is left free to combat it.

Thomas Jefferson

Democracy gives every man the right to be his own oppressor.

James Russell Lowell

Free government is founded on jealousy and not in confidence. . . . In questions of power, then, let no more be heard of confidence in man, but bind him down from mischief by the chains of the Constitution.

Thomas Jefferson

The qualities that get a man into power are not those that lead him, once established, to use power wisely.

Lyman Bryson

The hardest thing about any political campaign is how to win without proving that you are unworthy of winning.

Adlai Stevenson

A man of loose tongue, intemperate, trusting to tumult, leading the populace to mischief with empty words.

Euripides

Mountains culminate in peaks, and nations in men.

Jose Marti

The readiness "to do justly and to love mercy" springs from moral attitudes implanted early in life. But the attitudes aren't enough. We need some clues as to what constitutes justice and mercy in a confusing world. Those clues do not issue full-blown from the moral strivings of youth. They ripen slowly and not without cultivation.

D. Sutten

The imbecility of men is always inviting the impudence of power.

Ralph Waldo Emerson

Keep your course. Wax fat. Dishonor justice. You have power—now.

Aeschylus
(*in* Agamemnon, *the words of the leader of the chorus to Aegisthus*)

The only liberty I mean, is a liberty connected with order; that not only exists along with order and virtue, but which cannot exist at all without them.

Edmund Burke

Liberty is a need felt by a small class of people whom nature has endowed with nobler minds than the mass of men; . . . Consequently, it may be repressed with impunity. Equality, on the other hand, pleases the masses.

Napoleon Bonaparte

Mr. Auden's brand of amoralism is only possible if you are the kind of person who is always somewhere else when the trigger is pulled.

George Orwell
(commenting on W. H. Auden's use of the phrase
"necessary murder" in his poem "Spain")

Dulce bellum inexpertis.
War is sweet to those who have not experienced it.

Erasmus

Some people think that a person of integrity never sits out an honorable fight. But those doing the fighting know they have neither energy nor time to respond to all important challenges. They avoid some battles to throw strength into other battles, and-fight—whenever possible—on grounds of their own choosing.

D. Sutten

What are leaders for? Why do we need leaders in a free country? I would answer that the leader's function is to help determine, in any crisis, which of our possible selves will act.

Lyman Bryson

A leader is best
When people barely know that he exists,
Not so good when people obey and acclaim him,
Worse when they despise him.
"Fail to honor people,
They fail to honor you";
But of a good leader, who talks little,
When his work is done, his aim fulfilled,
They will all say, "We did this ourselves."

Lao-tzu

Love thy neighbor, but pull not down thy hedge.

John Ray

The spirit of liberty is the spirit which is not too sure that it is right; the spirit of liberty is the spirit which seeks to understand the minds of other men and women; the spirit of liberty is the spirit which weighs their interests alongside its own without bias; the spirit of liberty remembers that not even a sparrow falls to earth unheeded; the spirit of liberty is the spirit of Him who, nearly two thousand years ago, taught mankind that lesson it has never learned, but has never quite forgotten; that there may be a kingdom where the least shall be heard and considered side by side with the greatest.

Learned Hand

Experience should teach us to be most on our guard to protect liberty when the Government's purposes are beneficent. Men born to freedom are naturally alert to repel invasion of their liberty by evil-minded rulers. The greatest dangers to liberty lurk in insidious encroachment by men of zeal, well-meaning but without understanding.

Louis Brandeis

I believe there are more instances of the abridgement of the freedom of the people by gradual and silent encroachments of those in power than by violent and sudden usurpations.

James Madison

Those who expect to reap the blessings of freedom must, like men, undergo the fatigues of supporting it.

Thomas Paine

I don't know how democracy will end, but it cannot end
in a quiet old age.

Clemens von Metternich

No es lo mismo hablar de toros, que estar en el redondel.
It's not the same to talk of bulls, as to be in the bull ring.

Spanish proverb

When truth conquers with the help of 10,000 yelling men
—even supposing that that which is victorious is a truth:
with the form and manner of the victory a far greater untruth is victorious.

Sören Kierkegaard

Those who are engrossed in the rapid realization of an
extravagant hope tend to view facts as something base and
unclean. Facts are counterrevolutionary.

Eric Hoffer

Never forget that the nature of peace is commonly mis-
stated. Peace is not to be had by preventing aggression, for
it is always too late for that. Peace is to be had when people's antagonisms and antipathies are subject to the discipline of law and the decency of government.

   Do not try to save the world by loving thy neighbor; it
will only make him nervous. Save the world by respecting

thy neighbor's rights under law and insisting that he respect yours (under the same law).

E. B. White

The weakness of the fanatic is that those whom he fights
have a secret hold upon him; and to this weakness he and
his group finally succumb.

Paul Tillich

When I think thus of the law, I see a princess mightier than
she who once wrought at Bayeux, eternally weaving into
her web dim figures of the everlengthening past—figures
too dim to be noticed by the idle, too symbolic to be inter-
preted except by her pupils, but to the discerning eye dis-
closing every painful step and every world-shaking contest
by which mankind has worked and fought its way from
savage isolation to organic social life.

Oliver Wendell Holmes, Jr.

Les lois sont des toiles d'araignées à travers lesquelles pas-
sent les grosses mouches et où restent les petites.

Laws are spider webs through which the big flies pass and
the little ones get caught.

Honoré Balzac

I have always thought, from my earliest youth till now, that the greatest scourge an angry Heaven ever inflicted upon an ungrateful and a sinning people, was an ignorant, a corrupt, or a dependent Judiciary.

John Marshall
Virginia Constitutional Convention, 1829–30

If I were to ask you, gentlemen of the jury, what is the choicest fruit that grows upon the tree of English liberty, you would answer security under the law. If I were to ask the whole people of England, the return they looked for at the hands of government, for the burdens under which they bend to support it, I should still be answered, security under the law; or, in other words, an impartial administration of justice.

Thomas Erskine

The difference between a slave and a citizen is that a slave is subject to his master and a citizen to the laws. It may happen that the master is very gentle and the laws very harsh; that changes nothing. Everything lies in the distance between caprice and rule.

Simone Weil

Injustice is relatively easy to bear; it is justice that hurts.

H. L. Mencken

Democracy is still upon its trial. The civic genius of our people is its only bulwark, and neither laws nor monuments, neither battleships nor public libraries, nor great newspapers nor booming stock; neither mechanical invention nor political adroitness, nor churches nor universities nor civil service examinations can save us from degeneration if the inner mystery be lost. That mystery . . . consists in nothing but two common habits, two inveterate habits carried into public life—habits so homely that they lend themselves to no rhetorical expression, yet habits more precious, perhaps, than any that the human race has gained. . . . One of them is the habit of trained and disciplined good temper towards the opposite party when it fairly wins its innings. . . . The other is that of fierce and merciless resentment toward every man or set of men who break the public peace.

William James

Even if he were mediocre, there are a lot of mediocre judges and people and lawyers. They are entitled to a little representation, aren't they, and a little chance?

Senator Roman Hruska
(commenting on one of President Nixon's nominees
for the Supreme Court)

Judicial reform is no sport for the short-winded.

Arthur Vanderbilt

There is nothing more common, than to confound the terms of the American revolution with those of the late American war. The American war is over: but this is far from being the case with the American revolution. On the contrary, nothing but the first act of the great drama is closed. It remains yet to establish and perfect our new forms of government; and to prepare the principles, morals, and manners of our citizens, for these forms of government, after they are established and brought to perfection.

Benjamin Rush

Whoever conquers a free town and does not demolish it commits a great error, and may expect to be ruined himself; because whenever the citizens are disposed to revolt, they betake themselves of course to that blessed name of liberty, and the laws of their ancestors, which no length of time or kind usage whatever will be able to eradicate.

Niccolò Machiavelli

A State which dwarfs its men, in order that they may be more docile instruments in its hands even for beneficial purposes—will find that with small men no great thing can really be accomplished.

John Stuart Mill

At the extremes of the political spectrum one encounters people who are moved chiefly to find an outlet for the venom that is in them.

D. Sutten

To crush what is spiritual, moral, human—so to speak—in man, by specialising him; to form mere wheels of the great social machine, instead of perfect individuals; to make society and not conscience the centre of life, to enslave the soul to things, to de-personalise man, —this is the dominant drift of our epoch.

Amiel

To struggle against demagoguery scarcely fits the St. George-against-the-dragon myth so popular in folk lore. Our democratic St. George goes out rather reluctantly with armor awry. The struggle is confused; our knight wins by no clean thrust of lance or sword, but the dragon somehow poops out and decent democracy is victor.

Norman Thomas

In all institutions which are not ventilated by a keen draught of public criticism, an innocent corruption grows up like a toadstool (for example, in learned corporations and senates).

Friedrich Nietzsche

La plupart des hommes, en politique comme en tout, concluent des resultats de leur imprudence à la fermeté de leurs principes.

Most men, in politics as in everything, attribute the results of their imprudence to the firmness of their principles.

Benjamin Constant

Most government officials are rushing headlong to solve the problems of 50 years ago, with their ears assailed by the sound of snails whizzing by.

Eric Jonsson

I . . . regard the exaggerated hopes we attach to politics as the curse of our age, just as I regard moderation as one of our vanishing virtues.

Irving Kristol

You should never wear your best trousers when you go out to fight for liberty and truth.

Henrik Ibsen

The purpose of political action and the opportunity of free political life is for the people ultimately to determine their own destiny, and—after they have had the chance to learn —even to make their own mistakes. The great end they are serving is the development of their country through the development of themselves, not by authoritative interventions, no matter how competent or benevolent. It is not true that tyrants can never be benevolent. The trouble is that they go on being tyrants, and under tyranny individual men dry up for lack of spiritual exercise.

The purpose of a democratic society is to make great persons.

Lyman Bryson

When one knows of what man is capable, for better and for worse, one also knows that it is not the human being himself who must be protected but the possibilities he has within him—in other words, his freedom. I confess, insofar as I am concerned, that I cannot love all humanity except with a vast and somewhat abstract love. But I love a few men, living or dead, with such force and admiration that I am always eager to preserve in others what will someday perhaps make them resemble those I love. Freedom is nothing else but a chance to be better, whereas enslavement is a certainty of the worst.

Albert Camus

Individualism is a fruit of organized society. But there is no guarantee that it will survive or develop even in this soil. It is not the result of inaction or apathy. It is not a mere decomposition of society into its primitive constituents, or an atavistic reversal of the process of historical development. Like the artificial oasis redeemed from the desert, it must be perpetually irrigated. Nature has yielded it reluctantly, and seeks every opportunity to reclaim it. It is the most exquisite and fragile flower of that historic human enterprise which is called civilization.

Ralph Barton Perry

Nine-tenths of mankind are more afraid of violence than of anything else; and inconsistent moderation is always popular, because of all qualities it is the most opposite to violence.

Walter Bagehot

. . . that long roll of grim and bloody maxims which form the political code of all power.

Edmund Burke

EIGHTEEN

Today

"The Scene of the Accident"

The reports we get nowadays are those of men who have not gone to the scene of the accident, which is always farther inside one's head than it is convenient to penetrate without galoshes.

E. B. White

The only use of a knowledge of the past is to equip us for the present. No more deadly harm can be done to young minds than by depreciation of the present. The present contains all that there is. It is holy ground; for it is the past, and it is the future.

Alfred North Whitehead

For the revolution of modernity has not been only a material revolution but an intellectual revolution. It has been a moral revolution of extraordinary scope, a radical alteration in what the human imagination is prepared to envisage and demand. And it has changed the basic dimensions in which we measure happiness and unhappiness, success and failure.

Charles Frankel

On whatever pinnacles of release or success you may have hoped for, you will never hear a more subtle range of sounds than you can hear now, if you will only listen. . . . Never see a wider field of vision or more delicate structures or more subtle colors than you see now, if you will only be still and be aware.

John Platt

Our culture peculiarly honors the act of blaming, which it takes as the sign of virtue and intellect.

Lionel Trilling

Pessimism in our time is infinitely more respectable than optimism: the man who foresees peace, prosperity, and a decline in juvenile delinquency is a negligent and vacuous fellow. The man who foresees catastrophe has a gift of insight which insures that he will become a radio commentator, an editor of *Time* or go to Congress.

John Kenneth Galbraith

Most Americans are born drunk. . . . They have a sort of permanent intoxication from within, a sort of invisible champagne. . . . Americans do not need to drink to inspire them to do anything.

G. K. Chesterton

American life is a powerful solvent. It seems to neutralise every intellectual element, however tough and alien it may be, and to fuse it in the native goodwill, complacency, thoughtlessness, and optimism.

George Santayana

Democracy is liberty plus economic security. We Americans want to pray, think as we please—and eat regular.

Maury Maverick

There are two very bad things in this American land of ours, the worship of money and the worship of intellect. Both money and intellect are regarded as good in themselves, and you consequently see the possessor of either eager to display his possessions to the public, and win the public recognition of the fact. But intellect is as essentially *subordinate* a good as money is. It is good only as a minister and purveyor to right affections.

Henry James, Sr.

Isn't there something we can appear to be doing?

Henry Cabot Lodge
(in a letter to Theodore Roosevelt
during the 1902 coal strike)

Those who cannot miss an opportunity of saying a good thing . . . are not to be trusted with the management of any great question.

William Hazlitt

I am not quite sure what the advantage is in having a few more dollars to spend if the air is too dirty to breathe, the water too polluted to drink, the commuters are losing out in the struggle to get in and out of the city, the streets are filthy and the schools so bad that the young perhaps wisely stay away, and hoodlums roll citizens for some of the dollars they saved in the tax cut.

John Kenneth Galbraith

To get an idea of our fellow countrymen's miseries we have only to look at their pleasures.

George Eliot

In the land of lobelias and tennis flannels
The rabbit shall burrow and the thorn revisit,
The nettle shall flourish on the gravel court,
And the wind shall say: "Here were decent godless people:
Their only monument the asphalt road
And a thousand lost golf balls."

T. S. Eliot

The trouble with our times is that the future is not what it used to be.

Paul Valéry

[It] was not a superior quality of happiness that distinguished the pre-Ford, pre-radio, pre-boarding school home from our modern perches between migrations. . . . It was confidence . . . that made the great difference between then and now, a confidence that reached down below comfort or pleasure into stability itself.

Henry Seidel Canby

Nowadays we want our virtues embodied in the flesh and compounded with their opposites. Indeed, it is felt to be rather indecent to refer to them in public at all. The art of refined discourse now requires a dyslogistic vocabulary with which to make veiled allusions to virtue, as euphemisms were once required to avoid indelicate allusions to vice.

Ralph Barton Perry

If Jesus Christ were to come today, people would not even crucify him. They would ask him to dinner, and hear what he had to say, and make fun of it.

Thomas Carlyle

This gallant little eccentric seemed to have a disregard for human life that was 200 years out of date. But it could have been worse. He might have had a wholly modern disregard.

Geoffrey Household

What all the wise men promised has not happened, and
what all the damned fools said would happen has come to
pass.

Lord Melbourne

If movement and the quick succession of sensations and
ideas constitute life, here one lives a hundred fold more
than elsewhere; all is here circulation, motion, and boiling
agitation. Experiment follows experiment; enterprise suc-
ceeds to enterprise. . . . An irresistible current sweeps
away everything, grinds everything to powder, and de-
posits it again under new forms. Men change their houses,
their climate, their trade, their condition, their party, their
sect; the States change their laws, their officers, their con-
stitutions. . . . The existence of social order, in the bosom
of this whirlpool seems of miracle, an inexplicable anomaly.
One is tempted to think, that such a society, formed of
heterogeneous elements, brought together by chance, and
following each its own orbit according to the impulse of its
own caprice or interest,—one would think, that after rising for one moment to the heavens, like a water-spout,
such a society would inevitably fall flat in ruins the next;
such is not, however, its destiny.

Michel Chevalier
(speaking of the United States)

As a member of a society, the individual's pride and sense
of well-being are inevitably enhanced or diminished by the
purpose of his nation—what it stands for and where it is

going. If money and power, self-indulgence and self-protection are the goals of our society they will become the goals of its citizens, with damaging consequences. Nothing would do more for our national health than a feeling that we are engaged in enterprises touched with some kind of nobility or grandeur.

Richard Goodwin

America is a willingness of the heart.

F. Scott Fitzgerald

In the United States there is more space where nobody is than where anybody is. That is what makes America what it is.

Gertrude Stein

The Americans have passed from a state of barbarism to decadence, without the customary interim of civilization.

Comment of a Frenchman on the U.S.

When the Stranger says: "What is the meaning of this city?
Do you huddle close together because you love each other?"
What will you answer? "We all dwell together
To make money from each other"? or "This is a
    community"?

T. S. Eliot

You can't judge Hollywood by superficial impressions. After you get past the artificial tinsel you get down to the real tinsel.

Samuel Goldwyn

The Washington reflex: you discover a problem, throw money at it and hope somehow that it will go away.

Kenneth Keating

Manhattan, except for its harbor the least likely site for a modern metropolis, is an island tucked away on the map like an appendage on an anatomical chart. A hilly tract of mud, ledge, and fill, thirteen miles long and two miles wide, it is said to have been bought from the Indians for twenty-four dollars and a bottle of whiskey. Only now, after three centuries' experience, can one begin to appreciate the Indian's long view.

Jacques Barzun

It is the business of the future to be dangerous.

Alfred North Whitehead

To know the road ahead, ask those coming back.

Chinese proverb

No one knows the story of tomorrow's dawn.

African proverb

NINETEEN

Proverbs

"Too Clever Is Stupid"

~ ~ ~

Allzu klug ist dumm.
Too clever is stupid

German

If three people say you are an ass, put on a bridle.

Spanish

By the time the fool has learned the game, the players have dispersed.

African

Ser como el perico, que dice lo que sabe, pero no sabe lo que dice.
To be like the parakeet, that says what he knows but doesn't know what he says.

Spanish

Outside noisy, inside empty.

Chinese

Besser stumm als dumm.
Better silent than stupid.

German

There is no medicine for a fool.

Japanese

Para pendejo no se estudia.
To be a fool, one doesn't need to study.

Spanish

A palabras necias, orejas sordas.
To foolish words, deaf ears.

Spanish

No need to plant or cultivate fools; they grow everywhere.

Russian

He sheltered from the rain under the drain-pipe.

Persian

Many that go out for Wool, come home shorn.

Thomas Fuller

If Fools went not to Market, bad Wares would not be sold.

John Ray

All truths are not to be told.

George Herbert

He that would speak the truth must have one foot in the stirrup.

Turkish

Follow not truth too near the heels, lest it dash out thy teeth.

George Herbert

Veritas temporis filia.
Truth is the daughter of Time.

Latin

He that will steal an egg will steal an ox.

English

When the fox preaches, look to your geese.

German

De lo que veas cree muy poco,
De lo que te cuenten, nada.

Of what you see, believe very little,
Of what you are told, nothing.

Spanish

Qui s'excuse, s'accuse.
He who makes excuses, accuses himself.

French

Feather by feather the goose is plucked.

John Ray

You can't drive straight on a twisting lane.

Russian

Use your enemy's hand to catch a snake.

Persian

When its time has arrived, the prey comes to the hunter.

Persian

Old thieves make good jailers.

German

It's on the path you do not fear that the wild beast catches you.

African

No one tests the depth of a river with both feet.

African

No quiero el queso sino salir de la ratonera.
I don't want the cheese, I just want to get out of the trap.

Spanish

No se puede repicar y andar en la procesión.
One can't ring the bells and walk in the procession.

Spanish

If you try to be too sharp, you will cut yourself.

Italian

Ask a lot, but take what is offered.

Russian

The footprint of the owner is the best manure.

English

Si no puedes morder, no enseñes los dientes.
If you can't bite, don't show your teeth.

Spanish

If you want to clear the stream get the hog out of the spring.

American

If you want to keep your milk sweet, leave it in the cow.

African

It is na time to stoup when the head is off.

John Ray

Es sind nicht alle Köche, die lange Messer tragen.
They are not all cooks who carry long knives.

German

Whether the knife falls on the melon or the melon on the knife, the melon suffers.

African

If you would avoid suspicion, don't lace your shoes in a melon field.

Chinese

Amphora sub veste numquam portatur honeste.
A jug is never carried under one's coat for an honest reason.

Latin

When the cat and the mouse agree, the grocer is ruined.

Persian

For whom does the blind man's wife paint herself?

English

Make yourself into a sheep, and you'll meet a wolf nearby.

Russian

No medicine can cure a vulgar man.

Chinese

Del árbol caído, todos hacen leña.
Everyone makes kindling out of a fallen tree.

Spanish

A gato viejo, ratón tierno.
To the old cat, the tender mouse.

Spanish

Forgetting of a Wrong is mild Revenge.

Thomas Fuller

Every Tub must stand upon its own Bottom.

Thomas Fuller

The chiefe disease that reignes this yeare is folly.

George Herbert

The only cure for seasickness is to sit on the shady side of
an old brick church in the country.

English

Sub omni lapide scorpio dormit.
Under every stone sleeps a scorpion.

Latin

Keine Antwort ist auch eine Antwort.
No answer is also an answer.

German

The reverse side has also its reverse side.

Japanese

Primum non nocere.
First of all, do no harm.

Latin medical proverb

To spare the ravening leopard is an act of injustice to the
sheep.

Persian

Betters have their betters.

Japanese

Those near the temple make fun of the gods.

Chinese

He who carves the Buddha never worships him.

Chinese

No one teaches a cat how to look into a calabash.

African

No one shows a child the sky.

African

Hope is the poor man's bread.

George Herbert

En boca cerrada no entran moscas.
If you keep your mouth shut, the flies won't get in.

Spanish

Ewig ist ein langer Kauf.
Forever is a long bargain.

German

Index